LOVE NOTES
TO
FRIENDS & FAMILY

LOVE NOTES
TO
FRIENDS & FAMILY

JEAN CARLEY

TATE PUBLISHING
AND ENTERPRISES, LLC

Published by Tate Publishing & Enterprises, LLC

127 E. Trade Center Terrace | Mustang, Oklahoma 73064 USA
1.888.361.9473 | www.tatepublishing.com

Tate Publishing is committed to excellence in the publishing industry. The company reflects the philosophy established by the founders, based on Psalm 68:11,

"The Lord gave the word and great was the company of those who published it."

Book design copyright © 2013 by Tate Publishing, LLC. All rights reserved.
Cover design by Joel Uber
Interior design by Deborah Toling

Published in the United States of America

ISBN: 978-1-62746-673-8
1. Poetry / Subjects & Themes / Inspirational & Religious
2. Poetry / General
13.06.19

DEDICATION

This book is dedicated to Ken, Jr. and Renee who helped me stay on working terms with my computer, without which this book probably would never have happened.

ACKNOWLEDGMENTS

I will be forever thanking my Heavenly Father for my salvation, which can never be taken away, and for making me one of his children. I cannot imagine how it would be without His love and grace which has guided my life here on earth and helped me in troubled times. There have always been mountaintops at the end of life's trials and I thank Him for every one.

To my best friend and husband Ken, who has supported me over the years and encouraged my writing.

To Mike Winfree, my pastor, who is always there to offer encouragement, who leads his flock with love and compassion.

To the members of Oakland Baptist Church in Warner Robins, Georgia for the Christian love and companionship we share.

To my best friends who stand with me: Inez, Ted, Betty, Dave, Sharon, Nell, Allie, Joe, and Linda.

To members of my extended family who gave me insight to my ancestors and lineage, how this impacted my life, and which ultimately led to much of the contents of this book.

CONTENTS

Everyday Life

The Book 25

The Changing Days 27

I Am Not Old 29

There Was Always Joe 31

The Sun Always Shines 33

Things to Do 35

Shoes and Feet 37

A Way of Life 39

Cross on a Quilt 41

A View From The Window 42

God's Caretaker 44

The Days of Your Life 45

A Particular Day 46

How Many Mondays in a Week? 48

The Damp of "98" 50

Graduation Day 51

My Favorite Task 53

Safe Travels 54

Winning Battles 55

Thunder on the Horizon 56

Milk in My Coffee 57

Asking for Help..58
Day after Day 60
Buddy Talk 61
Street Corner 62
The Healing 64
Second Sunday 66
Foggy Weather Retirement...........................67
When I Falter...69
A Kiss 70
Life 72
Messages..73
Working Together..74
My Heart Hurts 75
Life's Special Days...76
Comfort...77
Friends...78
What Next? 79
Alone Today 81
He Can Handle It 82
Done..83
Coping...84
September Storms 85
Here Comes January......................................87
Waiting..89
Girlfriends 91
The Turning Point...92
A Sign 93
Countdown..94
To Virginia from Florida 96
Lost 98
Now...99

Grass in the Driveway 100
Easy Days 101
Fix This Mess... 103
Reading 104
Words 105
Winter Life 106
Spring... 107
The Paymaster... 108
All in a Day's Work 109
The Seasons Come... 111
Cottage Changes 112
The Answer.. 113
Phone Wreck... 114
Final Peace.. 115
Hugs and Surprises.. 116
Hurricane Charlie.. 117
Priorities 118
A Job Well Done 119
Hot Summertime 120
Getting Older with Grace 121
My White Crown... 122
A Good Day... 123
Where Were You?... 125
It Happened Again... 126
No Change in Twelve 127
Angel at My House 128
Extra... 129
T L C 130
What Is to Be 131
The Day After.. 132
Homework... 133

As Life Is Now 134
Spring Is Coming 136
Sunday Care 137
The Devil's Workshop 138
All Good Men 139
Old Barns-Old People 140
Your World 141
State of Affairs 142
A Wedding Prayer 144

∽

Fallen Heroes

Memorial Day 147
Heritage 148
Remember This Day 150
Pain and Peace 151
The Heroes of the Cole 152
The Honor of America 153
Remembrance of Nine-Eleven 154
Terror on Nine Eleven 155
The Eagle Cries 156
America the People 157
The Poppy Is Out Again 158
Remembrance 159
Memoriam for a Policeman 160
Storm at the Unknown 162
Those Who Don't Return 163
United States of America 165
The Tears of Memory 166
Wounded America 167

Nine from Nine Eleven 169
Justice for Nine Eleven 170

∽

Family

Someone Special.. 173
My Roots... 174
Cadbury Eggs 176
Sometimes 178
A Young Man's Life.. 180
Our Son... 182
A Gentle Man 184
A Father 185
The Completed Walk.. 187
To Honor a Mother.. 188
My Children.. 189
Visiting Angels.. 191
Mom's Flying Needles 193
Mothers and Children 195
Legacy of a Father 196
Call Waiting 197
South Dakota Snow.. 198
This Baby-A Gift.. 200
Birthdays 201
Good Day's Visit 202
Close By 203
Written Memories.. 204
What Friends Do 205
Love in a Word.. 206
Green Memory... 207

In Memory 208
More Than a Day 209
Everyday Things 210
Mother's Bible 211
They Were Here 212
Strength 213
Family 214
Field of Scenes 215
Envelope Power 216
Ask Only Once 217
Back Home Again 218
The Dog Tag 219

❧

God's Creatures

There Is That Bird 223
A Dog 225
Mother Nature 227
Cardinal Comfort 229

❧

Holiday Celebrations

A Season of Renewal 233
Kids and Christmas 235
Resolutions 237
Thanks 238
The Trip 240
The Christmas Cards 241
The Wearing of the Bells 243

He Is Not There...244
Our Celebration 246
Overshadowed 247
The Christmas Card...248
Turkey Day 249
America's Veterans...251
The Coming Year 253
Happy Birthday Jesus 254
The Lily 255
The Fourth of Ninety-Nine 256
Allegiance...257
A Season of Thanks 258
The Message 260
Because It's Christmas..261
Busy–Busy 262
Here It Comes...263
A Son Not His Own 264
Hearts and Love..265
Things to Do...266
Just to Remember 267
It Has Been Told 268
The Coming Year...270
After the Cold 271
My Jesus Lives...272
Words to Thank 273
A Christmas to Remember..................................274
Peace in the Year...275
Signs of the Times...276
Christmas Gift 277
Joy..278
It Feels Like Christmas 279

In the Middle 280
This Year 281
Gifts of the Christmas Child 282
Next Year to Come 284
Every Christmas 286
This Year to Another 287
After the First Day 288
The Holiday Cones 289
Thank You Father 290
Cactus Season 291
The Face of Christmas 292
Part of the Celebration 293
Wish Me Merry Christmas 294
This Year to Come 295
Seven/Four/Seven 296
Duty of the Fourth 297
Memories 298
The Flag of the Fourth 299
Georgia Thanksgiving 300
It Was Told 301
Together 302
Thanksgiving's History 303
Christmas—A Story 305
Sunday Sunrise 306
The Fourth of Twenty Ten 307
Peace on Thanksgiving Day 308
Christmas This Year 309
Resurrection 311
A Day to Honor 312
Stories to Tell 313
To Be Thankful 315

Special People

Coming Home..319
The Leaving...321
The Privilege of Camelot 322
A Joy for Living..324
A Place to Go 326
Laura's Prayer...327
The Healer's Touch 328
Rose on a Lamp..329
Your Presence..330
Distant Friends...331
A Man of God—A Legacy.............................332
The Gipper's Journey 334
The Folded Cloth..336
God Goes to a Ball Game 337
The Preacher 338
Who God Blesses 339
Old Friends 340
The Patriot Guard...341
The Lifetime of a Veteran 342

Walking with the Lord

My Lord and I...345
The Search 347
Protection 349
Waiting for His Message 350

The Way to Work..351
The Passing Storm 352
The Scales of Your Life 353
The Cross...354
Never 355
The Peaceful Word...357
Smiling Angels 358
You Have Always Been There 359
The Meeting Place 361
The Saving Day..362
Who Is This Church 363
What Would Jesus Do 365
The Gift..366
What Would Love Do.......................................367
Things 369
Open for Business..370
Great Benefits..371
The Answer..372
Taking Care 373
A Box of Memories 374
The Quiet Cross...375
God with Us 376
The Healing 377
Computer on Loan 378
Anna's Door...379
Part of a Task...380
Commandments 381
Cross Beauty..382
Lost in the Valley...383
As the Lily Grows 384
Arc over the Cloud 385

The Shepherd's Care 386
The Christ 388
Again 389
Path of a Church 390
Katrina's Wrath 392
Just How Many 393
Daily 394
God's CO 395
Faith's Legacy 396
That's How My Heart Writes 398
Of Late 399
Hearts Far Away 400
The Master's Card 402
Prayer List 404
Moving Into Fall 405
Psalm 91 406
A Place and Time 407
Where I Am Now 408
The Sunday Sermon 409
A Picture Taken 411
On Election Day 412
Back Home Again 413
Background Workers 414
Thoughts of Things 415
Weather in a Doughnut Hole 416

PREFACE

When I started keeping the contents of this book, I never envisioned I would ever publish. Over the years my friends would read something I had written and would ask me why I did not find a publisher but it just never seemed important.

My original intent in writing was simply to lighten the burden for a friend or say something which would make their day better and help them to realize that through it all God was standing next to them and would not let them fall.

I have been influenced by events could have brought our country to its knees but instead it has survived and as a people we will not admit defeat. There are those among us who do not have the option to fail and will hold their communities close and claim victory by the hands of our Heavenly Father.

I have been influenced by family members who did not give up in the face of adversity, in essence turned it into an example of just how to live their lives as an example to others.

A few years ago I made a promise that if this book published any profit would go to my church and I plan to stand by that promise. You cannot make a bargain with the Heavenly Father, but if you stand by a promise you will succeed. And if you are secure in your faith the outcome will be accepted and you will move forward. More than ever of late I have known that this was never "my book", and that it was to be His message and I will turn any proceeds over to my church. I am still amazed that He used me to put these "words on paper", and that if you find something that puts your heart at ease and gives you comfort that was my intent all along.

Whether or not this venture succeeds is entirely up to the Lord. I know in my heart He gave me the talent and the ability to use it for His purpose, and I will accept whatever outcome He sees fit. It is my sincere wish that by reading this book you will realize just how important it is to walk with the Lord on a daily basis, and let Him guide your life in a manner that will bring honor to Him.

EVERYDAY LIFE

THE BOOK

I do not know what got me started,
On the road to write this book.
It's just seemed one day it happened.
A thought sent from God is all it took.

There have been times when I wanted to say,
Something to help or comfort someone.
But no matter how hard I would try,
Somehow the words just would not come.

I would carry a burden on my heart,
Trying to find a word or phrase to say.
Then I would give up and walk away,
Knowing I had to wait yet another day.

I had to see it was not I who needed to speak,
And I did not yet have the words to say.
I must simply wait on him to let me know,
When it was time he would lead the way.

I have a peace within whenever I write.
I do not always know what will come.
But I know I am blessed by my Lord,
And whatever it is, his will is always done.

If by reading what I have written here,
You find quiet comfort or peace and rest.
Then you must thank the Lord above,
It is through him you and I am truly blest.

THE CHANGING DAYS

Today was the first of a brand-new season.
Bright, beautiful, fresh and clear.
I'm sure that many more will come,
But each of God's days are special here.

Today was the first of a brand-new season.
White fluffy clouds are found.
The sun was brighter than in days before.
Everything is quiet, not even a sound.

Today was the first of a brand-new season.
Everything is waiting for its own time.
As if everything somehow should stop,
So some special event can fall in line.

Today was the first of a brand-new season.
Open all the doors and let the fresh air in.
The house will smell so clean and fresh,
Like a peaceful shelter where He has been.

Today was the first of a brand-new season.
Now things will start to move so very fast.
Holidays are coming, families will gather.
We will soon feel wintertime's cool blast.

Then there will be spring and summer to come.
Things happen as the world continues its turn.
The sun will move to its new place.
The seasons change, God's work is not done.

Everything is in order, I can deal with that.

I AM NOT OLD

I'm not old.
I am barely seventy-two, that is not old.
I act a little experienced that is because I am.

I'm not old.
The Lord gave me gray hair when
I was still in my teens.
Gray hair does not make me old; per-
sonally, I think it's pretty.

I'm not old.
My children are grown and away from home.
That does not make me old, just better.

I'm not old.
With God's help we raised them well.
We can be proud.

I'm not old.
I fit into the workplace and do
my job better than most.
I am dependable, that does not make me old.

I'm not old.
I still have a lot of living to do; we will travel.

I'm not old.
Just because I give advice, rock babies,
and make good cookies,
Does not make me old, just needed.

I'm not old.
I have a definite place in this society; I can fill it well.
And you will know I have been
there. I am proud of that.

I'm not old.
In my Lord, I am forever young; He
can use me to his advantage.
He is not through with me yet;
how can I possibly be old?

THERE WAS ALWAYS JOE

There was always Joe.
Who made you feel welcome,
And helped you become a val-
ued member of the community.

There was always Joe.
There to put you back on track when you were angry,
About something over which you had no control.

There was always Joe.
There to give you advice when
you were too hardheaded
To see the forest for the trees.

There was always Joe
Who thought he was really ask-
ing a favor for you to watch Gayle.
Boy did that dog ever have him trained.

There was always Joe,
Who understood that you enjoyed just loving his dog,
Because you appreciated what he did by adopting her.

There was always Joe,
Who teased you about babysitting your bird,
And then used the opportunity to
teach him how to whistle.

There was always Joe.
Who had good ideas on how to
do things so the quality,
Would be better than good enough
for government work.

There was always Joe
Who helped his wife raise children who
will be respected by their peers.
A man who was a credit to his faith
although it was different than yours.

There will always be a Joe.
Whose memory will not leave us anytime soon.
We will remember him and feel his presence,
And we will be blessed for having known him.

There will always be a Joe.
Somewhere in our everyday life we
will run across one of them.
Every now and then, we are just one short right now.
There will always be a Joe.
We will have to make do, but then
we have the Lord to help us,
And Joe will be watching.

THE SUN ALWAYS SHINES

Even on the darkest day, it's still shining.
You just can't see it, that's faith.
It is supposed to be that way.

The sun always shines.
When the clouds go away, there it is.
Just as bright as before.
It is supposed to be that way.

The sun always shines.
It lets us know of the Almighty Father and
His infinite control over everything.
It is supposed to be that way.

The sun always shines.
No matter what man will say,
Some things will not change.
It is supposed to be that way.

The sun always shines.
When the heart is broken, the sun shines.
It warms you, soothes you, and strengthens you.
It is supposed to be that way.

The sun always shines.
I used to tell my children this when they were young;
That tomorrow is a brand-new day.
It is supposed to be that way.

The sun always shines.
It's only one of the ways God tells us I love you.
It is supposed to be that way.

THINGS TO DO

There are so many things for me to do.
Things to fix, adjustments to make.
When I go to sleep, they are on my mind.
I'll try to find the time when I awake.

There are so many things for me to do.
Somehow I must find order in my day.
New things were added when I awoke.
Somehow there has to be a better way.

There are so many things for me to do.
Some are necessary to finish my day.
Some are important to see me through.
Need to find a way to stretch me out.

There are so many things for me to do.
I think I just have to get them fixed.
But then, would that be better?
Thought I was doing well with what I had.

There are so many things for me to do.
Do this here, that there, did I do that?
Who said I had to? Why right now?
Guess I'm not the only one in this mess.

There are so many things for me to do.
I must have a better plan.
Has one even been invented yet?
Someone should have told me so.

There are so many things for me to do.
Do you think God could make an adjustment?
No, he did it right the first time.
He will just have to help me; I'm sure he will!

SHOES AND FEET

There are some days when things will
fall apart, no matter what.
Things get hectic, you're going
under, where do you start?
You will find the light at the end of the tunnel.
Just don't wear new shoes to work.

Take it easy, slip off those shoes under
your desk, who will know?
Answer the phone and talk to a few,
jump up, put on your shoes.
Do the best you can to get through the day.
Just don't wear new shoes to work.

Lunchtime may come, but you will
stay in, too much to do.
You do this and then do that, get some-
thing going to make it right.
Get up from your desk and take a
break, get a cup of coffee.
Just don't wear new shoes to work.

Afternoon is here, you've done your
best, and things fall in place.
But how your feet do hurt, in fact
they are almost numb.
Don't watch the clock that will do
no good, keep on working.
Just don't wear new shoes to work.

The day is done, you are homeward
bound, look forward to the time.
The car seat is pure comfort, wind
in your face, the radio eases.
Getting home brings joy to your soul,
a warm cup of coffee waits.
Just don't wear new shoes to work.

A WAY OF LIFE

I am a diary farmer's daughter, raised on a farm.
Early to rise with work to do before the light of day.
It was the Masters' plan that we be there.
Trusted with his creatures to help us make our way.

I am a diary farmer's daughter, raised on a farm.
Blessed with a caring fam-
ily to keep me safe from harm.
Loving parents, a brother, and sis-
ters all shared my world.
Sheltered by a home built with care, safe and warm.

I am a diary farmer's daughter, raised on a farm.
Something to be proud of, a solid rock foundation.
A way of life known only by a fortunate few.
Given the responsibility to pro-
vide for others in our world.

I am a diary farmer's daughter, raised on a farm.
With love in my heart, valuable to me, I am proud.
A heritage that is not found in
many people in this day.

I am a diary farmers' daughter, raised on a farm.
Taught to be respectful and show concern for others.
Who might be less fortunate or need a guiding hand;
A sweet smile or special look and a gentle touch.

I am a diary farmer's daugh-
ter who remembers the farm.
The lessons learned, the values taught, the good times.
The lean years with love and support abounding.
Prepared to handle anything life would send my way.

That life is over; a new one has been wonderful for me.
The memories I have will be treasured forever.
I will share them with you if you
ask; they are in my heart.
They are part of my soul and of this God approves.

CROSS ON A QUILT

Quilts are made with warmth in mind,
For someone you love or to fill a need,
For a special purpose of a personal note,
Something to last for years to come.

Quilts are made with warmth in mind.
Not to be hidden away from admiring eyes,
But to bring one's face into view.
Something to last for years to come.

Quilts are made with warmth in mind,
Like the one that graces the wall.
It represents a labor of love.
Something to last for years to come.

Quilts are made with warmth in mind.
This one represents a union of hearts.
A coming together, which makes us as one.
Something to last for years to come.

Quilts are made with warmth in mind.
We are so glad the cross is there,
And everything for which it stands.
Something to last for years to come.

A VIEW FROM THE WINDOW

Things are busting out all over the place.
The lily will bloom in a day or two.
The gourds will decorate the fence.
The days will soon be long and warm.

Things are busting out all over the place.
The ginger plants are coming up.
The cattails are ready to be picked.
Some already grace my back porch.

Things are busting out all over the place.
Spring is in the air, but days are still cool.
The ducks have hatched their babies.
The water will soon be gone.

Things are busting out all over the place
The palms from Easter now live on my porch.
We lost a lot of trees this time around.
But the grass seems to be so much greener.

Things are busting out all over the place.
We still have work to do in the yard.
Make up my mind to plant some flowers.
Hold a good thought is all we can do.

Things are busting out all over the place.
Another season is here for us to enjoy.
A place to sit and look out the window.
A warm cup of coffee makes it right.

God is in control here, I can deal with that.

GOD'S CARETAKER

This is written to comfort you,
To let you know I really care.
Your burden is not yours alone,
For part of it I will share.

This is written to comfort you,
To tell you what's on my heart.
I have an arrangement with my Lord.
He will take the largest part.

This is written to comfort you,
To remove pain from your heart.
You are such a caring daughter.
You've done more than your part.

This is written to comfort you,
You see, I struggled just the same.
I have been where you are today,
Then quietly Jesus called my name.

He will hold you, bless you,
And touch your heart with love.
All of this to help you through,
With blessings from above.

THE DAYS OF YOUR LIFE

The days of your new life are about to start.
The old you will now put away.
Some things will not change for you.
But every morning will bring a happier day.

The days of your new life are about to start.
Everything before has led up to this day.
God with infinite care has brought you here,
Now you should let him lead the way.

The days of your new life are about to start.
So many changes will happen so fast.
But the Lord will always be with you.
And now he has found love for you at last.

The days of your new life are about to start.
You will not make earthly decisions alone.
Now you have a shoulder to lean on.
You have chosen each other to be that one.

The days of your new life are about to start.
And for both of you our prayers are one.
Enjoy each other; love and live your new life.
Let your Lord be the head of your home.

A PARTICULAR DAY

This particular day.
Like most, it starts by man's clock.
Either I am awake or it wakes me.

This particular day,
A cup of coffee, the dog is up,
And needs to go outside

This particular day.
The bird is uncovered or else he fusses.
The dog is barking at the door to get in.

This particular day.
Sunshine streams through the kitchen window.
Almost too bright but welcome.

This particular day.
It may be Friday, if so, sleep in tomorrow.
Or a Saturday, do Saturday's work.

This particular day.
It may be Sunday; God's day, slow and easy
Read the paper, get ready for church.

This particular day.
Sunday, go to church, worship God in song and word.
Get programmed to handle the upcoming days.

This is a particular day!

HOW MANY MONDAYS
IN A WEEK?

Today was one of those days.
My umbrella got stuck in the door,
And dumped water all over me.
I started early and ended up late.
Guess what? It's only Monday.

Today was one of those days.
Got out of bed, tripped over the dog.
Danced a lot but landed on my feet.
Did not know I could move like that.
Guess what? It's only Tuesday.

Today was one of those days.
It's hump day, middle of the week.
Made up my mind things will be okay.
Split my knee on my desk again.
Guess what? It's only Wednesday.

Today was one of those days.
Things are really looking up.
Four down, only one more to go.
Things will get better, I know.
Guess what? It's only Thursday.

Today was one of those days.
I really like my job, you know.
Sometimes the work is not too swift.
All you have to do is make the four.
Guess what? It's Friday.

How long until five o'clock?

THE DAMP OF "98"

FLOODED YARD

O.K., already, I'll become a duck.
It would be the safer thing to be.
After all there's plenty of water.
There's plenty of company for me.

My feet have become one big wrinkle.
And the forecast continues to be bleak.
And even if we owned a boat,
With our luck it would probably leak.

And then there is the wind that blows.
Which is responsible for bringing rain?
Every time I go outside it does my hair.
When will the sun ever shine again?

All this because of dumb El Niño.
Could be we've been left in the dark?
God promised no more flood.
But did Noah build another ark?

If he did, where's my ticket?

GRADUATION DAY

Today's the day you should be proud of.
The worry and sweat that got you through.
Just don't forget the road you traveled,
And the one who walked along with you.

You always acquire wisdom when older,
When you have learned by your mistakes.
You must always find the best way for you,
And the joy your accomplishment makes.

You are traveling where others have been,
But your path is now your own to make.
Those who know you are happy and proud.
Best wishes and praises you should take.

Always guard your outlook on this life.
Mark the road down which you walk.
Then be willing to guide someone else,
And always be willing to listen and talk.

MY FAVORITE TASK

I often wonder if the day will come,
When I will no longer write.
But then a word or phrase,
Will come to me like a light.

I am often amazed at what I write.
I have no way to ever know,
What will be said to you and me.
I wait on Him for the words to flow.

I often feel the message is for me;
Something I need to do or know.
And it's His way of telling me,
How things are supposed to go.

Sometimes I'm just not happy,
With the way the words turn out.
I may have to change it so it works,
But in the end there is no doubt.

He always takes His time with me,
And His presence I understand.
What you may read on this paper,
Is often Jesus using my hand.

I never knew I had this talent,
Until one day it came to pass.
And as long as He allows me,
I will enjoy my favorite task.

SAFE TRAVELS

Thank you, Lord, You've done it again.
Taken care of something I asked of You.
It must be because of our arrangement,
    You'll take care of us if I ask You to.

Thank you, Lord, You've done it again,
Keeping him safe and taking care of things.
While we are apart I will miss his touch.
But I know the contentment Your love brings.

Thank you, Lord, You've done it again.
As said before, we are safe from all harm.
You will always be there; I need only ask.
I will simply rest in Your loving arms.

Thank you, Lord, You've done it again.
I am content, and my life is good.
You have everything under control,
Just like I always knew You could.

WINNING BATTLES

Things happen that are not important.
They should not cause me to complain.
I must look on the brighter side.
I can do this if I will call on His name.

I must simply pray for His leading.
Look to other things to occupy my mind.
No good can be accomplished,
By letting bad feelings waste my time.

I must not utter unkind words in haste.
I must learn to wait and bide my time.
Because only He can take the hurt away,
And give me back my peace of mind.

By doing this I will always be for the better.
Those who hurt will not triumph in the end.
With Jesus helping and giving comfort,
There is no doubt that He and I will win.

THUNDER ON THE HORIZON

My life is good, and I am happy.
Everything is falling into line.
Each new day is always different.
I am happy just to wait for God's time.

My job is going pretty good.
I still haven't trained the boss.
But as long as I keep hanging in there,
The time invested will not be lost.

Life at home is smooth and sweet.
Too many blessings for me to list.
My dog is happy and glad to see me.
She always lets me know I'm missed.

My family all seem to be doing well.
We are close though many miles apart.
I hear from then on a regular basis.
I hold on to each of them with my heart.

All of this stuff is good, thank you.
So I should not be one to complain
I am happy; this is the way it is to be,
But, Lord, we could sure use some rain!

MILK IN MY COFFEE

It is a peaceful Sunday afternoon,
Fresh and clean after the passing storm.
All in all it has been kinda nice,
Two days apart from the weekday norm.

It didn't start out all that good you see.
Friday things were in not a bed of clover.
Everything just seemed to get worse.
I was not in control, and the bad took over.

I let little things, which are not important,
Become stumbling blocks along the way.
They made me angry at the one I love,
When he had done nothing to ruin my day.

Saturday came up so bright and pleasant,
A good cup of coffee and a new day to see.
Because someone thoughtful, before I rose,
Simply had a quart of milk waiting for me.

It doesn't take much to turn things around.
It is done when we let Him lead the way.
Most of the time it is what we do with it,
When we just remember who made the day.

ASKING FOR HELP

There are days things are not as they should be.
Your mind knows something is just not right.
You're not real sure how you should fix it.
Like somehow you are not walking in the light.

Thinking back, all sorts of things come to mind.
Of what you should or should not have done or said.
It's sometimes just too late to go back and fix it.
You're just spinning wheels, not able to get ahead.

I guess we will all sometimes have days like this.
You are uneasy, and you feel all alone and sad.
You just want everything to hurry and get better.
And you want to fix it so you don't feel so bad.

It is not the Lord's intent that we be unhappy.
It is to be His message that will show the way.
To let us know how we are to make it right.
It could be simply "I love you" will make the day.

Whatever it is, when the message comes through,
You will be able to figure how to take care of it.
Make that the most important thing that you do.
Then you will have peace of mind and spirit.

My prayer will be that you will find direction.
And what you accomplish will give you rest.
And the peace that you are searching for,
Will come knowing you have done your best.

DAY AFTER DAY

Things will happen that are good and bad.
We must learn to take them in stride.
Like this bruised and aching foot of mine.
Black and blue my stocking will not hide.

Like days when the boss is out of town.,
And many things for him we must handle.
We'll get it done and then all will be fine.
Just so we don't burn both ends of the candle.

Then there are days when things just break,
And then we have to say little prayers.
God please make the hot water heater work.
Believe me I do not like taking cold showers.
Sometimes you just feel so overwhelmed.
Things just pile up, one on top of the other.
You do not know which way you should go.
Maybe just jump in bed and pull up the cover.

But a message comes through loud and clear.
Just do not let the little things get you down.
I am always here just to take care of you.
Just call my name, I can always be found.

BUDDY TALK

My buddy is always there for me.
Lots of things at work we share.
Family, friends, and daily things.
Lots of good ideas always there.

My buddy always has time for me,
When things get really hectic.
He puts order back in things,
That way I don't go ballistic.

My buddy is always there for me,
Even when I tend to wander.
He brings me back safe and sound,
And keeps me from going under.

My buddy is always there for me,
When situations get really bad.
We can look back on this time,
And remember the talks we had.

So for you, my friend, I write this.
It's what needed to be said.
Thanks for being willing to listen,
When I needed to clear my head.

STREET CORNER

Today I hugged a friend of mine.
Happily, for the whole world to see.
We hadn't seen each other for a while.
My friend was really glad to see me.

We talked a while there on the corner,
Of all the things that this life has dealt.
How we still miss each other's smile.
The companionship we still felt.

All at once there was no hurry.
Everything came down to a quiet time.
We could talk and cure some wrongs,
That life had put on this friend of mine.

He and I have parted on our journey.
We may never meet this way again.
But it was wonderful just to see him.
Just to tell the world he is my friend.

There were times we prayed together.
For things that were heavy on my heart.
We cared what happened to each other.
Always our life will share that part.

What happened may be scorned by some.
This affection between me and my friend.
You see his skin is of a different color.
Even today some wrongs do not mend.

THE HEALING

The wrong has already been done.
We cannot ever take it away.
We only have the choice to forgive.
Like it or not, that is God's way.

We are not allowed to be the judge.
The choice is not ours to make.
If he has asked for God's pardon,
Vengeance will not be ours to take

This is God's answer to prayer.
After forgiveness, it is put away.
Never to be brought up again.
God will deal with it in His own way.

It does no good to continue the pain,
Of what this country's going through.
Just get on with your daily lives,
And to your own selves be true.

If you allow this to make you angry.
Then you will be the one to lose.
Just remember the end result.
Will depend on which you choose.

Just put your trust in one who knows,
The best way for this to be ended.
The best way for this to end
Let Him take care of everything.
Only then will our wounds mend
Only then will our wounds be mended.

SECOND SUNDAY

Today was such a wonderful day.
We just about filled every pew.
Decisions were made for Jesus.
And some lives will begin anew.

Today we ran out of bulletins.
And though I spelled it wrong,
We still were able to worship,
In truth, and prayer, and song.

Today we got such good news,
Of vows and promises of love.
A new family has now begun,
With blessings from God above.

Hugs and handshakes all around.
Our love for each other is so sweet.
He was with us here in this place today.
It will continue each time we meet.

FOGGY WEATHER RETIREMENT

I guess the day has finally come,
When there's not much to write about.
There have been no major revelations.
Could be that God has tuned me out.

The weather has been pretty good.
We have escaped another storm.
Outside today is pea-soup fog,
But inside we are safe and warm.

Things at home are safe and secure.
The family is well though far away.
This will be my last year to work.
Now I'm looking to retirement day.

I feel I have crossed over a bridge,
Now that boss knows the day will come.
It's funny how your life will change.
Right after something has been done.

We can have the things we worked for.
A new part of life will now begin.
We can enjoy our kids and family,
And feel His peace from deep within.

Friends will stay close and support me.
Peace and contentment will be mine.
Now I just have to be content and wait.
All good things will happen in His time.

WHEN I FALTER

There are those days when I seem to falter.
Doing things for which I feel remorse.
Knowing that if I had just thought it out,
I would have chosen a different course.

If I ask for His forgiveness, it will come,
So I can again walk in His light.
It is Him I have wronged most of all,
And with Him I must make it right.

I know there is much to thank Him for.
This is to be my most important task.
I must ever praise His loving name.
When I want Him near, I need only ask.

So pray for me in my time of trial.
That as His lamb He will safely hold me.
And I will find the peace that I need.
And from this burden be set free.

A KISS

Last night I stood in church and touched a child.
A soft loving caress to her pretty blond hair.
It was nothing really, just something I often do.
A gesture to let children know I really care.

I dismissed it from my mind and went on my way.
Then I saw her looking as me as if for a sign.
Maybe trying to find the answer to a question.
Still somehow it did not register in my mind.

I was talking to other people who were there.
Discussing what we needed to get done.
How to get upcoming events taken care of.
Which task could be handled by which one.

Then I felt her arms go around my waist.
And her face turned up with a loving smile.
We stood there holding on to each other.
We moved away from the world for a while.

Then it dawned on me as I was standing there.
What kind of reward could be better than this.
What on this earth could my Lord give to me.
When I bent down and my cheek felt her kiss.

I am a mother, and my children I dearly love.
I am blessed by my Lord each and every day.
And He always lets me know I am important.
Maybe this was just another of his special ways.

LIFE

I have been blessed in so many ways,
Too many for me to ever tell.
When I stand back and look at life,
I am surprised I have done so well.

There is no way I could ever deserve,
The wonderful life He has given me.
But by His Grace my life is filled,
And in His care I will always be.

You see I know that through it all,
I have had a loving wonderful friend.
Who has kept me safe and secure,
And He will be with me until the end.

MESSAGES

If I don't do it now, it won't get done.
The messages that the Lord will send.
So He doesn't have to tell me again.
I guess He wants me to stop right then.

They come to me at different times.
You would be surprised what I've lost.
By not writing it down right then.
Not helping someone has been the cost.

That is how it is in our lives you see.
It should be done as soon as you know.
If you don't, chances may not come back.
Then what will your life's record show?

There is a time and place for everything.
He has set them all in order to be done.
It will never be our lot to ask questions.
If you know about it, then you are the one.

Do not think that you have to wait on him.
If He lives in your heart, He will lead you.
He will show the pathway you are to take.
And always be with you to see it through.

WORKING TOGETHER

Thank you for the pretty flowers.
They brightened up the whole room.
Sitting on my desk for all to see.
Orchids, roses, carnations in bloom.

People who came to call saw them.
They said you must think I'm great.
I told them it takes a super "boss."
And a secretary to keep him straight.

When we all work together as a team.
There is no telling what we can do.
So we'll get back to normal on Monday.
The week of celebration will be through.

Every day I am thankful for all of you.
You put up with me, and we get it done.
We each have a down side in what we do.
But the end result is the important one.

MY HEART HURTS

There is this ever-present burden,
That has been lying on my heart.
God tells me I need to ask for His help,
And He has told me where to start.

It has been here for quite a while.
Something only He can help me do.
I will constantly pray for His guidance,
And I now ask for prayers from you.

Keep me in thoughts and on your mind,
That He will give me patience and love.
And the opportunity that I will need,
Because it can only come from above.

Someday I will come and speak to you,
To tell you it has been taken care of.
And will then be happy together,
Knowing in the end it was by His love.

LIFE'S SPECIAL DAYS

GRADUATION

Life is moving so fast for you right now
Wonderful things are happening every day
This birthday will be one of those memories
It will sty with you as you make your way.

Looking back on life helps find the future,
And where you are, and what you should do.
Always guard your outlook on this life.
It helps to find the pathway best for you.

Accept true friendship when it is offered.
Learn how to accept advice from those
Who have been where you will be going.
Taking responsibility for the life you chose.

Making decisions will give you satisfaction.
Always be willing to learn from your mistakes.
Then you can accept all the wonderful rewards,
That hard work and accomplishment makes.

There are those who love and care for you.
They have given to you from their very souls.
Make sure you never forget who they are.
Because of them, you will reach your goals.

COMFORT

I write this to comfort you,
While you look for the Master's light.
I know that he is never far from you.
He will lead you through the night.

I write this to comfort you.
To let you know I really care.
Your burden is not yours alone.
For part of it I will share.

This is written to comfort you.
To tell you what's on my heart.
I have an arrangement with My Lord.
He will take the largest part.

Jesus will hold you, guide you,
And touch your heart with love.
All of this to help you through,
With blessings from above.

FRIENDS

Thank you so much for allowing me to share,
What I find on my heart that I must say.
My pleasure is to be a beacon for loved ones.
Hoping in some way it brightens their day.

I can tell you that you are often on my mind.
There is something that bonds us as friends,
And we can find a comfort in each other.
Let it always be the message that the Lord sends.

I can only be humbled by the task I am given.
So as my friend, do not let me be too bold.
Feel free to call me back if you need to.
Pray that the Lord will keep me in His fold.

If by your reading messages I have written,
You can find a place for your soul to rest.
Then you must always thank the Lord.
It is through Him that we are truly blessed.

WHAT NEXT?

Last year this time we did not know.
What we could do about the smoke.
The fires were raging all about.
This year we suffer from the soak.

Last year we were covered with ashes.
It was hard to catch a breath of air.
This year we're looking for a boat.
And praying for a day that's fair.

We had our scare a few months ago,
And we started to pray for rain.
All of a sudden we found ourselves
Hoping the sun would shine again.

My dog looks up before she leaves.
From the safety found under the bed.
She steps outside, the thunder claps.
She thinks she'll pee later instead.

I planted flowers in my backyard.
I do not think they're gonna grow.
They probably went the other way.
Decided in China they will grow.

With all respect to powers that be.
I think we've been left in the dark.
Maybe we should call Noah back.
And let him build another ark.

ALONE TODAY

Today you are lonely in your heart.
Just a little more than yesterday.
An emptiness that's hard to fill.
Your best friend has gone away.

You are left alone with memories,
Of whom he was and what he did.
The times he pulled you through.
On his shoulder your tears were hid.

And there was his happy laughter.
Often with an impish grin on his face.
It will always be held in your memory.
Secure in your heart's special place.

Please find comfort in what he was,
To you, his children and his friends.
His presence will always be there.
It will be a legacy that does not end.

Tomorrow the sun will be on your face.
What has happened was by His plan.
It will not be your place to know why.
Just allow Jesus to hold your hand.

HE CAN HANDLE IT

A part of another's life needs to be changed.
 I just don't know how it is to be done.
 It must be that it is not in my control,
And that the Father will have to be the one.

It is one of those things always on my mind.
Not ever knowing what the outcome will be.
 I just must be patient and wait on God.
 When it is time He will show it to me.

I feel there may be something I could do,
 And there are many times I have prayed.
 But yet the answer does not come to me.
I guess He knows why it has been delayed.

I pray the outcome will cause no one pain.
That one day it will just be taken care of.
 And I can then find the peace I need.
Knowing it was done His way and by His love.

So it is my place of just watch and wait,
 And be patient for the answer to come.
I must not try to figure how it will happen.
Just rest in Jesus knowing it will be done.

DONE

Somehow it always gets done in the end.
We realized this over the last few days.
He was again here to take care of us.
He did it in one of His wonderful ways.

He was riding along with us you see,
As we were going about our daily task.
He took care of us and kept us safe.
He just does it; we don't have to ask.

And now we have been able to tell others.
How good He is and how He will always care.
There is no way we could ever pay Him for,
The comfort of knowing He is always there.

Tomorrow we will start another journey.
His loving care will comfort and surround.
He will take care of us because we are His.
Under His angels wings we will be found.

COPING

The sun came up again today.
Things are in order as they should be.
There may be a problem on my heart,
But Jesus will be there to comfort me.

I must handle things as they come.
To worry about the future is a sin.
I must learn that He is in control,
And my burden I should give to Him.

I must accept that things will happen,
In His time frame and for His reason.
It shall not be my place to know why.
Things will come to be in due season.

But having the frailties that I do,
It is often hard for me to understand.
That Jesus will accept me anyway,
If I will just do the best that I can.

I must allow this to be my comfort.
He is watching over me and mine.
He will pull them from the valley,
And give them peace all in good time.

SEPTEMBER STORMS

RUNNING FROM STORMS

They came in all through the night.
Searching for a safe place to stay.
Caring people were there to greet them.
Tomorrow would be a better day.

They settled in and started to wait.
Not knowing what they would find,
When they returned to their homes.
They watched and listened for a sign.

Then it came to them, the happy news.
The storm had passed by out to sea.
Now they would pack up and go home.
Prayers were answered for you and me.

There are those who still are suffering.
Who have lost everything they own.
They cannot seem to find God's peace.
It is if they have been left all alone.

But He is still there and cares for them.
They only need to call out in prayer.
He can lead them where they need to be,
And give them comfort for this hour.

It shall be our calling to pray for them.
What has happened I know not why.
But you can be assured of this,
It is but for the grace of God go I.

HERE COMES JANUARY

RETIREMENT

Today's the day I gave them the date,
When it will be my last day here.
I made it official this morning.
Now there is no mistake, it's clear.

It is just another door I will go through,
That I have chosen to be right for me.
This is a time to look forward to.
From the workday week I will be free.

This is what I have worked hard for,
And up until now I have paid my dues.
Some were good and some were bad,
But it was always what I would choose.

This is such a happy time in my life,
As my friends feel this joy with me,
And wish me well as I go my way.
I know this is what was meant to be.

I can always come back for a visit,
To check and see that you are well.
When I come back there will be stories,
That it will do my heart good to tell.

So wish me well and pray for me.
That we will travel safe and secure.
The world out there waits for us.
Ready or not we are coming for sure.

WAITING

The days are getting shorter.
The time is winding down.
It will not be very long now.
Retirement I will have found.

There will be days of leisure.
I just may not get out of bed.
Or I'll just sit around all day,
Not caring who or what is said.

I've been putting off little things,
That I just did not have time to do.
I may have time to go help others,
Or I may just stop and think of you.

No matter what I'll take my time.
I do not intend to get involved.
I will not ever have to hurry.
Take one thing and get it solved.

Along about May we will start to go,
To see all the places we want to see.
We will not answer to a clock.
There will be no place we have to be.

Please be happy for us.
This is what we want to do
Just think of all the things I'll find,
To write about and send back to you.

GIRLFRIENDS

I'm writing this 'cause you're my friend.
I could use a few more like you.
You're one I enjoy visiting with.
Since you're one of a treasured few.

Today we're having lunch in town,
Accomplished after several tries.
Looking back on what we've shared,
Good and bad, just how time flies.

We each have such busy lives,
Each expecting changes to come.
We have lots of things to talk about,
With just an hour to get it done.

Girlfriends are a special lot,
Sharing things we can't with others.
It's kinda like a special place.
It's different than sisters and brothers.

This is a good thing we have started.
We must make an effort to continue it.
We can always meet in friendship.
If not in body, certainly in our spirit.

THE TURNING POINT

We sometimes find ourselves moving.
On roads we don't need to travel.
It is our choice whether it is smooth,
Or dangerous like slippery gravel.

We can always call on our Lord,
When we have doubts or fears.
How we handle what He tells us,
Decides if it ends in peace or tears.

Then there are times we just don't listen,
And we get further and further adrift,
From the fold that He has made for us.
Guarded by grace, which is our gift.

Jesus always wants you to remember,
When the road you travel leads you astray,
And you are headed in the wrong direction.
You can make it right, He shows the way.

A SIGN

A good thing has come to be for us.
Our church's sign went up yesterday.
We all did our part to see it done.
For a lost one it may show the way.

We were standing around in the dark,
Finishing up what had to be done.
With only the headlights from a truck,
The switch was thrown, and it was on.

We hugged and held on to each other.
The time was right, and it was good.
We went into Your house to thank you.
How it came together was understood.

We are a body of the Father's children.
We were put here by our Father's design.
We will always welcome into His house.
The ones who come because of a sign.

COUNTDOWN

Well here I am the week before.
By all accounts I am on my way.
It won't take very much for me,
To get ready for retirement day.

I'm looking forward to lazy days,
With nothing much to do.
Just lay in there sleeping late.
If you want I will think of you.

It's not any great revelation,
I've been planning this for years.
The way I got to where I am,
Is by a lot of blood, sweat, and tears.

Please do not expect a lot from me.
I do not want to disappoint you.
I will be in control of my life.
Handling it the way I want to.

If my Lord has something for me.
He will show me all the ways.
That I can use to help someone.
I will let him guide my days.

I will not have to live by a clock.
I will learn to decline with tact.
I may not be there when you call.
Leave a message, and I'll get back.

TO VIRGINIA FROM FLORIDA

Outside today the sky looks like Virginia.
If I were there, I would look for snow.
This time of year it would be cold.
Maybe not a place I would want to go.

But there are times when I am homesick,
For the friends and family still there.
That's where most of my memories are.
If I visited with them, we would share.

As time goes by all things will change.
When I go back it will not be the same.
But that is where I will be later this year.
Looking for those who share my name.

Returning to a place in the mountains,
Where wonderful summer days are found.
Simply content to watch the world go by.
By the Shenandoah, a special sound.

I can go there and be content for days.
Just alone and at peace in that place.
Allowing nature to show me the way.
Letting my life move at a slower pace.

But as it is with me this particular day.
I will allow my mind to do the walking.
I can put my pleasant thoughts on paper.
By allowing my pen to do the talking.

LOST

I know I put it somewhere.
But where I just don't know.
Looking all over this house,
Hoping somehow it will show.

There are only so many places,
That it could be in this place
I have looked in all of them.
Waiting for it to show its face.

Things like this make you crazy.
You think you're losing your mind.
It's just got to be here somewhere.
With any luck you'll be able to find.

It's not that it can't be replaced.
You just wanted to fix it today.
It didn't cost you all that much,
But without it there is no way.

This really should be no big thing.
I should be able to just walk away.
It is really not all that important.
I can wait and do it another day.

I just know it's here somewhere!

NOW

There are so many great little things,
That now I have time to see.
It's like they were not there before,
But have been put here just for me.

Like today I saw how blue the sky is.
How a breeze will gently move a tree.
I saw how high a bird could soar.
An example of what it is to be free.

I realized how softly a day would go,
Now that I have time to just stand still.
To see it as part of an eternal picture,
And how it comes together at His will.

This was not a luxury I could enjoy.
I did not have time to stop and see.
I had places to go and things to do.
I had things that were expected of me.

Now my life goes down a different road.
One that I would like to share with you.
I'll check with you from time to time,
So you will know my dreams came true.

GRASS IN THE DRIVEWAY

RETIREMENT

I am enjoying the quiet, slow, easy days.
No great rush or project to do anyhow.
I am able to plan each day as it comes.
There are things I can do, but not just now.

I am able to watch things around me,
Where I didn't have the time before.
We are making plans not cut in stone,
So we can enjoy them all the more.

I find more contentment every day.
When it comes to the things I do.
I stop to see what needs to be done,
And I now have time to listen to you.

I'm finding new places to put things.
Then sometimes I move them back.
I will do things the way I want to.
Around here nobody's keeping track

I do not always have to be somewhere.
My car can now sit still for days on end.
I'll just let the grass grow in the driveway.
When I'm ready, I'll look around the bend.

EASY DAYS

There's not a lot going on around here.
But that's just fine with me today.
I'll just take things as they come.
I can wait for God to show the way.

Outside it is a warm and sunny day.
There is nothing special for me to do.
This must be what retirement means.
I would wish this for each of you.

Tomorrow will be another Monday.
But I won't have anywhere to go.
It's something I've enjoyed of late.
That hard work paid for, so I can know

I will not forget who put me here,
And wherever He wants me to be.
There is always a message to be told.
Something there He wants me to see.

So I would want to be ever watchful.
Maybe I can help to guide someone.
When time comes to enjoy their years.
Then get direction from what I have done.

FIX THIS MESS

People are ganging up on me around here.
It's gotten to be more than I can handle.
I pray for this one and then someone else.
I'm about to burn both ends of the candle.

First there's the prayer for my girlfriend.
Trust me she needs all the help she can get.
And there are always people from my church.
Somehow, I have just not caught up yet.

Then there's the pastor who needs attention.
Don't know what to do to get him well!
First one thing with him and then another.
What will happen next, no one can tell.

I guess we all get too busy in this life.
We must learn to stop long enough to ask,
For Jesus to help us take care of all this.
For Him it will not be such a big task.

So everyone should take time and remember.
Just to make this a very special Sunday.
Use it as it was intended, for rest and prayer,
And then Jesus can make it a better Monday.

Knowing God He will probably throw in some
Extra stuff just for good measure, he usually does.

READING

Most people don't like to read poetry.
They always find other things to do.
It's something they do not understand
And the message does not get through.

Mostly they just don't have the time.
To see what's in the written word.
Or they think it's not meant for them.
They're more attune to what is heard.

You can always try to find a purpose,
In things that people may have meant
Sometimes it may be a personal thing.
Or just a message that needs to be sent

It is much like reading God's Word.
It's something you must want to do.
It takes time, and you need His help.
For the true meaning to come to you.

We all have a lot to learn every day.
There is a book that has all we need.
Keep God's Word out on life's table.
Always there when you need to feed.

WORDS

Tonight I read some of what I wrote.
Amazing how the words comforted me.
Some of the things I now find on paper,
Were put there just for my heart to see.

I live a pretty ordinary life you see.
Not always a lot going on around here.
But there are messages to be found,
From my Lord just for me to hear.

At the time they were written for others.
Maybe telling of experiences I had known.
In some small way to comfort a heart,
So a healing seed could be sown.

Or maybe they were written to tell a story.
Just to remind us of what we often forget.
How He constantly loves and cares for us.
How the pathway of our lives is to be set.

Even now as prayers are answered every day,
And I spend more time praising His name.
Let me ever show my joy to those I meet,
That someone else's heart may have the same.

WINTER LIFE

It's not really all that good a day you see.
It's awfully cold and windy outside.
Try as I might my spirit is still low.
Like I need to go somewhere and hide.

It's been that way for several days now.
I think of things I need to try to forget.
They are just there in the back of my mind.
Try as I might I can't let go just yet.

I try to keep busy, but it's just not easy.
Time makes my memory bring it back.
I just have to ask for help to handle this.
I must get past the devil's attack.

Right now I need to get things in order,
So life can return to what it was before.
Happy and healthy and working for Him,
With a happy heart to praise Him more.

Sometimes when I write it gets better.
Maybe that will happen again this time.
God gave me this talent to use for Him.
I pray He will give me peace of mind.

SPRING

It's been one of those busy days you have,
When there are lots of things you need to do.
There is work in the yard because its spring.
To get it like you want it, the job falls to you.

There are errands that come at week's end.
You work them in along with the other stuff.
So that when your day is done and you rest,
You hope everything was done well enough.

In your mind each is a piece of God's work,
As you patiently wait for the plants to grow.
There will be weeds to pull, fertilizer to spread,
And with God's help their beauty will show.

There is a never-ending list of things to do.
If not yours, you help someone else with theirs.
You water the grass because there is no rain.
You hold out a hope when a cloud appears.

We have been given a place to live down here.
It is only ours because of God's infinite grace.
There is a joy we derive from the work we do,
So that in our little corner, it is a better place.

THE PAYMASTER

I have this job that's mine to do,
And I'm learning a lot as I go.
Like the best way to get it done,
So peace of mind we will know.

Trying to make less for someone else,
So pastor can take care of other things.
Filing things so there is some order,
When it's done the satisfaction it brings.

I do not wish to impress anyone here.
I just want to do what needs to be.
I want no person's praise of accolades
I know he appreciates this from me.

I have no worry how I will be paid.
Jesus is the paymaster every day.
He's the one I will be working for.
Things are right when He leads the way.

ALL IN A DAY'S WORK

Saturday came early as they sometimes do.
We would see what happened as it came to be.
Then it was decided he would go to church.
He wanted it nice on Sunday for all to see.

The day started cool so it would be better.
There were weeds to cut and a walk to trim.
I knew when he finished he would be tired.
He accepted the work; it was expected of him.

So he cut the weeds, and he trimmed the walk,
He was covered in green from head to toe.
But it looked so nice around God's house.
It was done and satisfaction he would know.

He came home, replaced his shoes and socks.
With a can of coke, and a football game on TV,
We talked about things we had planned to do,
But they could wait for another day to see.

So I planned my errands for the rest of the day.
Then he said let's get started on your shelf.
Even as tired as he was after his day's work,
He was willing to put what I wanted before self.

He cut the board, and we worked on the pieces.
Now it will soon be on our wall for all to see.
It will remind me of a day he worked with pride.
First time for his God and then time for me.

THE SEASONS COME

A few days ago I was again reminded,
That man does not have a rhyme or reason.
That all things as we think they should be,
After all still move in God's time and season.

I cannot explain why bad things happen.
Why many know such suffering and pain.
While some are sheltered and held apart.
Why some of us know loss and others gain.

Here in my world I am thankful to my Father.
That He has kept me and mine safe from harm.
I can find peace and comfort in my faith in Him.
He always shelters me, and I feel safe and warm.

Outside I can see the seasons are changing.
Even now as leaves fall and life slows down.
I am reminded that celebrations draw near,
That thanks will be given and new joy found.

My Christmas cactus is full of new buds.
It will bloom early in the next week or so.
It will show beauty that only God can make.
It is God's time for this beauty to show.

COTTAGE CHANGES

There have been some changes around here.
Our house is not just like it used to be.
This change is good; it's what we wanted.
One change is outside for our friends to see.

When we moved here, we loved the peach.
We liked the porch and the fenced-in yard.
We moved in and made it our new home.
The changes we've made were not so hard.

The first we decided was to paint the peach.
We thought we would like to try it white.
We did this and stood back to take a look.
That was good thing, and it looked just right.

The back porch needed major construction.
We had an idea of what we wanted to do.
We did not know what we might find.
But we plowed right in and saw it through.

Now we've changed the whole appearance.
We totally changed the way it will look.
Instead of a house, it looks like a cottage.
Whoever said we had to go by the book?

THE ANSWER

There are so many ways for us,
To fix things that causes us pain.
Friends and family can comfort.
God's Word is there time and again.

But having the frailties that we do,
We try to muddle along to get it done.
We worry and let it change our lives.
In the end Satan has always won.

We take our stress out on loved ones.
But they don't know what to say.
All they want to do is offer their help,
As they try to make it a better day.

In the end it is always so senseless.
The way we will worry and complain.
When all we have to do is ask him,
And He will be there once again.

You just don't have to deal with it.
You can leave it with the Lord tonight,
He's going to be up all night anyway.
It won't take Him long to make it right.

PHONE WRECK

When I saw the car in front of me,
I knew it was not going to stop.
The light was out at the intersection.
He did not even notice the cop.

In my mind it is as if in slow motion.
I saw two cars start to twist and bend.
The collision, scattered metal and glass.
Broken bodies that would never mend.

A policeman came and asked of me.
Was I absolutely sure what I would say?
He has to make an investigation you see,
To protect the one directing their way.

Where was I going, and where was my car?
What did I see; who did I think was right?
Where were the cars before it happened?
Were both vehicles always in my sight?

I can remember the things I told him.
The driver in front of me was alone.
A family with kids was in the other car.
The driver in front of me was on the phone!

FINAL PEACE

I've tried for days on end to find a message.
Something from my heart to ease your pain.
But try as I might it did not come to me.
I went through my book time and again.

So what you will find following this page.
Are things I have written over the years.
They were for another time and place.
Perhaps meant to ease someone else's fears.

But you must know my heart cares for you.
You have been constantly on my mind.
You see I know what you are going through.
In my time I too found peace hard to find.

But in the end I found that God really cares.
He gave me strength to do my very best.
And when it was over I knew in my soul.
I answered only to Him and I was at rest.

HUGS AND SURPRISES

There always will be things we remember.
Most of the good stuff is little surprises.
You never know when to expect them.
Funny sometimes how an occasion arises.

Most of the time it is a series of events.
You never know just how it will end.
Sometimes it's when you need it most.
Can be something you share with a friend.

They may not know they made you smile.
For them it is the normal thing to do.
It may be something they did on a whim.
Let them know how much it meant to you.

It does not have to be money or riches.
These things always fall by the way.
But feelings expressed from their hearts
Will be remembered for many a day.

Nothing means as much as genuine caring.
Something to be cherished for a lifetime.
Like a simple hug to express an emotion.
This is special memory, yours and mine.

HURRICANE CHARLIE

We had known for days he would be coming.
We just did not know where he would land.
Then we were told he would move to the west.
At the last minute we found he was at hand.

We had little time to get things safe and secure.
Our windows to board and yard stuff to hide.
Then we went inside to wait out the storm.
We would pray for safety and God to abide.

There are those who lost all earthly possessions.
For them I am sorry, but their lives were spared.
They must now remember that in the storm.
Our God was with them and He surely cared.

So many strangers are now here to help us.
They clear trees, restore power, working late.
They are setting poles and fixing telephones.
Every chance I get I tell them I appreciate.

Our home was spared, and we are safe today.
But so many around us did not fare as well.
Now we have a chance to do good in His name.
It will keep us busy, and we have a story to tell.

PRIORITIES

Today I have one burning question,
That has lingered on my heart for days.
Why do we spend taxpayer earnings
In extravagant and unnecessary ways?

We have fighting men on foreign soil.
In a war that some men say should not be.
They do not have things they need most.
In order to make this land ultimately free.

They do not have support from their leader.
He is too busy doing other things today.
He will celebrate in comfort and safety.
While they struggle in a land far away.

There will be galas that will cost millions,
Yet our men lack what they need to survive.
They pull metal pieces from garbage dumps
To armor their vehicles in order to stay alive.

I believe in my country and for what it stands.
I will raise my flag and pray for these good men.
I just hope our leaders do what needs to be done.
So blessed peace will come, then and only then.

A JOB WELL DONE

We have reached a milestone in our church,
And now we are well on our way.
With joy in our hearts and peace of mind,
Tomorrow can only be a better day.

The county has approved all our hard work.
What we set out to do, we did with pride.
Now all we have to do is finish the course.
It will be done with love from inside.

The fun and laughter God allowed us to have,
As we worked toward the goal day after day.
We learned what joy accomplishment brings,
And how things just fall in place along the way.

The work was hard but it was worth every bit,
Of the aching muscles and exhaustion every night.
The promise of tomorrow's things to be done,
And changes we needed just to make it right.

We will soon have it completed for all to see,
How people can pull together to get it done.
How obstacles can fall by the wayside.
With our Father's help the battles are won.

HOT SUMMERTIME

This time of the year is just not the best.
It's just to blasted hot around this place.
I go outside to do just one simple task,
And I have water running down my face.

My back porch is not mine to enjoy today.
It is nice and pretty there, the plants are fine.
But if I venture out with my coffee cup,
I'm back in the house in double time.

The humidity sticks, and my hair goes frizzy.
I have shed all the clothes the law will let.
But I have to be decent, you just never know,
Who will come by to visit or something to get.

Only the things that can be done in the house,
Will get my attention on days like this.
I know this is where we chose to retire,
Yet so much of my Virginia I still miss.

So I will make the best of where I am right now,
Because this is where God wants me to be.
I will just look forward to the winter months,
For cool nights and better days that I will see.

GETTING OLDER
WITH GRACE

It's been a couple of busy weeks around here.
It's a major effort just to keep him feeling good.
I don't know what's gotten into this man.
Whatever had been suggested, boy he would.

But then some things must be left up to one,
When they are uncomfortable or sick.
One does not know what another feels,
And choices are not always yours to pick.

I am very aware of the fact that I am sixty-five,
And I will never feel the youth I once knew.
And for all that has happened to me in this life,
I feel blessed because I am here with you.

But God is good, and I am at peace with life.
There is no better time to be than right now.
I've done the best with what He gave me,
And I still have more to do for Him anyhow.

MY WHITE CROWN

While out walking alone this afternoon,
Someone commented on my white hair.
That it was like a crown that I wore well,
That it was beautiful, natural white and fair.

But when I thought of what my friend had said,
About this crown God has given me to wear.
I was flattered that she thought me worthy,
And what she said certainly I should share.

I thought then of all that we take for granted.
The things God does for us all along the way.
He watches over us, shelters and protects.
And gives us all we need each and every day.

Like most earthly possessions we often neglect,
We do not give them the honor they deserve.
We do not make them a tool for His honor,
And use them when given the chance to serve.

My Father has promised us crowns to wear.
And I hope He will give me at least one or two.
And that I will be able to lay them at His feet.
For my dear Lord it shall be what I must do.

A GOOD DAY

Today was one of those good days.
Early this morning we helped a friend,
Then we took care of a honey-do task.
Something to replace, we could not mend.

We enjoyed an intelligent conversation,
With someone who needed our advice.
On how to help someone they knew,
Recalling life's experiences can be nice.

Then there was the afternoon walk,
The breeze was gentle, talk was good.
It was a time of good communication.
Some things unsaid are just understood.

On our way, we dropped in on a neighbor,
And talked of their raising a little one.
We realized just how different it is today.
But with God's help they will get it done.

A friend came to visit later in the day.
He stopped by on his way somewhere.
Nothing much to talk about, just a chat.
A good thing, he knows we really care.

Just another day in the run of things.
This is how a good life is supposed to be.
Just getting along and helping each other,
Brings God's contentment to you and me.

WHERE WERE YOU?

Where were the parents of this young man,
When he purposely loaded his gun?
And before anyone knew what happened,
Four people were shot, the deed was done.

Did they not know their child was troubled?
Did they even take an interest in their son?
Did they have any idea what he was doing?
Or too busy to know he had taken the gun.

Just where else can we find the reason why,
That four innocent people were shot today?
By a young man so troubled he lost control.
His parents were not there to show the way.

As if that were not sufficient for pause,
We may never know why this came to be.
For deep in the corners of his troubled mind,
There was a cause the world may never see.

And that is not the end of this wrenching story.
At fourteen years old he took his own life.
We cringe at the mark he made on this world.
Another cut to our hearts with a killer's knife.

IT HAPPENED AGAIN

Somewhere else the gunfire rang out.
And innocents fell in a blast of hate.
Randomly chose to pay the reaper;
No time to escape; it was just too late.

There should be something we can do.
Such sadness in my heart I have never known.
What is gained by the numbing heartbreak?
Which never heals for those left alone.

This time of peace has been shattered.
It will be hard to celebrate a joyous season.
To go onward will be more than they can do.
For some life will have no rhyme or reason.

How do you explain to a questioning child?
Why someone they love is not there anymore.
How do you keep others from trying to find,
Some horrendous way to even the score?

Where will it ever end? What can we do?
Is there no safe place for our people to go?
It is out of our hands; we can only watch.
While we pray for our Lord to take us through.

NO CHANGE IN TWELVE

Not a lot of change in two thousand twelve.
God will still take care of me and mine.
As we walk and talk with Him every day,
I am sure everything will be just fine.

We have a lot of work to do for Him,
Just like we have in years gone by.
That is where we find our satisfaction.
Just doing good things, not asking why.

There are things we need from our Father,
That will never change from day to day.
Are always there and we don't have to ask.
His grace and love helps us find our way.

It may be that I must expect and wait,
For the chance to help my fellow man.
There may be something that I can do,
At a special time when no one else can.

That is what He always does for me,
And I am blessed to let you know,
That some things just do not change,
And that His love through me will show.

ANGEL AT MY HOUSE

A STATUE

An angel came to my house,
And has found a watching place.
She is tall and has regal bearing.
Representing the Father's grace.

She is of such an infinite beauty.
Love was in the hands of her maker.
And that determined the end result,
That God allowed me to be her taker.

She guards the flag of my father.
Up on the mantle for all to see.
She may have been made by man,
But she means much more to me.

I will pass her on with Dad's legacy.
She will be part of my family's story.
And those who will come to own her,
Can imagine her likeness in Glory.

She reminds me He is always near,
And always cares for me and mine.
I only need to call on His name,
And contentment is there to find.

EXTRA

There has been an extra person here today.
I thought I felt him riding on my shoulder.
I knew I could probably work around him.
I asked for God's help; it made me bolder.

By end of day all things will be in order.
You see I only have one I need to please.
At home I will find a warm cup of coffee.
I can put my feet up and enjoy the ease.

I will not have to worry about this day.
It has been recorded in the Book of Life.
I know that God is pleased with the entry.
He knows how I handled the day's strife.

Now I know He was the One on my shoulder,
And when I asked for help, He was there.
He chased away what was testing my life,
And I could finish my day without a care.

You just have to let Him take over your day,
And things will get better as you go along.
After all He just wants to walk with you.
He will consider your thanks a joyful song.

Another day the devil lost!

T L C

A year ago I abandoned the flowerpots.
Where I put them, it was just too hot to grow.
So I moved them to the back of the house.
What I would do with them I did not know.

They just kind of sat there by the back door.
We cut around them, just not knowing.
If I just wait, a purpose will come to be.
I saw some green, something was growing.

It got taller and I started to watch it grow.
It looked like a weed struggling there.
The only water was from God above.
Was this the message He would share?

I do not know where the flower came from.
It is not something I would have planted.
Yet it is beautiful there all alone at the door.
A single little flower, a new life, God granted.

Today I gave it water as I passed by the door.
It seems brighter and happy to be there.
Like most things in life you will find today.
All they need is a little tender loving care.

WHAT IS TO BE

I must not allow myself to get discouraged,
Although God already knows what is to be.
I must put my trust in Him as I continue,
Knowing in my heart He will take care of me.

But then there are those that I care about.
I am constantly praying for them every day.
Hoping in my heart He will give them safety,
And their faith will be renewed along the way.

I worry that they do not feel His presence,
And have no assurance that He is there.
That nothing will keep them safe from harm,
And when things are bad, no one will care.

Things may change as they travel life's path,
When they will know contentment and peace.
That will come when Jesus enters their heart.
And trials they know on earth will cease.

I cannot imagine this life without my Lord,
And I search for words to tell those I love.
Just how wonderful their life could be,
Sheltered in the arms of the Lord above.

THE DAY AFTER

2008 ELECTION

Yesterday I did what I thought was best.
Today the world will not be the same.
But life will go on and all will be well.
Prayers and petitions are in His name.

You see there is no winner or loser.
We are required to pray for this man.
So choices he makes for our nation,
Will be led by the Master's hand.

Do not despair if you did not win.
This is how God wanted it to be.
If there is a lesson to be learned,
He is the teacher for you and me.

Our life will not change that much.
We still have everyday things to do.
We are still the land of the free.
Its okay, God will take care of you.

Fly your flag and be really proud.
For a right not to be taken away.
That the United States of America,
Is still a beacon that shows the way.

HOMEWORK

Things have begun to get quiet around this place.
I do not know if I will be able to handle this.
Until now there was always something to do.
I have to stop and wonder; what did I miss?

All of a sudden it's down to some little stuff.
Just to top off what we started some time back.
The things that take more time to get ready to do,
That somehow always ends up in the leftover stack.

I must say my yard is a vision to behold.
Only one or two more trips will be needed.
There are some things we cannot seem to fix.
Is there a yard that does not need to be weeded?

The inside of the house is what I envisioned.
Neighbors ask if we do work outside the home.
With lots of help from my mate, it is completed.
And I tell these people that they are on their own.

I got on the trusty computer this morning,
Just to figure how much we might have spent.
At the friendly neighborhood Lowe's store,
My budget is not broke, but it's really bent.

AS LIFE IS NOW

There are lots of things I've learned in life,
And most of them I have used for my good.
But some were hard for me to stick to,
No matter how much I knew I should.

Like the Lord always tells me not to worry,
And I really try to turn things over to Him.
And most of the time I manage to get it done,
But then my mind still goes back to them.

There are things I do that give me satisfaction,
Like stepping to the bar to see something done.
Because in my heart, it is the right thing to do,
And if no one else will, then I will be the one.

I have never been content to accept failure,
And I have been known to go the extra mile.
If in the end good has been accomplished,
I can be satisfied just by someone's smile.

Nothing impresses me more than integrity,
Especially when shown by someone I know.
Nothing gets better than standing with a friend,
To make our world better than it was before.

Pray for something you need every day.
Do not ever give up on what prayer can do.
One by one things can change for the better,
Then in the end it was partly because of you.

SPRING IS COMING

This time of year I start to wonder.
But I know spring will soon get here,
It is just a matter of time until it comes,
Some things still happen to have no fear.

The grass is still brown and dead.
But my lilies are keeping their pace,
I've even planted some new ones,
Out back in a sunny brand-new place.

My rosebush has a new home this year;
In a corner of the fence where it can grow,
Without being constantly cut back.
Now its red beauty can safely show.

The pup still gets his daily walk.
His clock goes off early every day.
He makes his journey around the block,
Where he wants to go, he knows the way.

Today the sun is bright and it's a good day.
Things to do will be taken care of.
If we will just patiently wait on Him.
As the day goes, He will show His love.

SUNDAY CARE

I'm up most days before the paper comes.
We must be on the end of her route.
The dog still sleeps but husband is awake.
I'll get the day going there is no doubt.

On Sunday morning it's an easy task.
I can take my time to get it done.
I work around things that don't move.
Out the front window I find the rising sun.

A quiet time to see if anyone wrote,
A message that I might need to read.
I'll reach above the desk for God's word,
To see if there's something I need to heed.

By this time the cup of coffee kicks in,
Even though I find it is suddenly cold.
I'll go back to the pot to get some new,
But by then it is bitter and tastes too old.

There will be a certain amount of wonder,
About the day that's about to be.
How He gets me up and gets me going,
And thankful He still takes care of me.

THE DEVIL'S WORKSHOP

Today I watched them burn my flag,
That our soldiers would bleed and die for.
And we are the hand that feeds them.
This is enough! Why should we do more?

No matter how we try, it will not work.
When we leave things will be the same.
We cannot win this battle for any good.
They demonstrate and curse our name.

The god they worship is ugly and false.
Peace and love they may never know.
It has been this way thousands of years.
Can't we just back off and let them go?

Or maybe we must just stay and fight.
Maybe we just try to hold our ground.
But how will we ever win this battle,
When there is no future to be found?

I can see an underlying core of evil,
That now shows its ugly vicious soul.
And there is no way we can tame it,
No matter how grand might be our goal.

ALL GOOD MEN

Now is the time for all good men,
To come to the aid of their country.
If we do not do something soon,
It will not be a country that's free.

You have the chance to make it right.
If you are ever going to do it, it's now.
If you ask for guidance from above,
Perhaps God will show you how.

First you need to ask direction from Him,
And follow the lead He will give you.
You just may learn something here.
We will need his help to see it through.

You just may have to change your mind,
About how things will need to be done.
Do not make up your mind too early.
It may not be easy to pick the right one.

Our country was founded by men of God,
Now God must find one that will lead
Get us back to where we need to be
And then remember His message to heed.

OLD BARNS-OLD PEOPLE

I found a beautiful story this morning,
And then I compared it to our lives.
We are now at an age where beauty,
Is often found though others eyes.

I remember the barn I grew up with.
Part of it still stands in its glory.
These are memories I will never forget.
That barn is a part of my life's story.

There were things there I grew up with.
Some of them are in my home to stay,
And now they are a part of my life.
Our daughter will have them someday.

Sometimes we have to look for beauty,
In things we have known for a lifetime.
Just don't let go of the important things.
We can leave them for others to find.

YOUR WORLD

Your world just came crashing down,
You think it may never again be whole.
And you can only stand by and watch,
You are broken to your very soul.

Now stop and look at what you have.
God is walking right by your side.
He has never left you and never will.
Your broken heart has a place to hide.

Your friends will love and care for you.
Know this pain they would gladly bear.
It will make your load easier to carry,
Just by knowing they will be there.

There is a brighter day awaiting,
As you walk in this valley of tears.
We know it will be there for you,
As it has been for all of your years.

You will feel His very presence,
If the answer you do not understand.
He will hold you as you go your way.
Safe and secure in the palm of His hand.

STATE OF AFFAIRS

Am I better off than I was last year?
I am afraid I would have to say no.
I'm still looking for promises made.
There is no improvement to show.

Our leader takes credit for the good,
With which he had nothing to do.
The end to the life of a terrorist,
Had been planned before he knew.

All the changes we will need to see,
Will be done by the common man.
Who got up every day and worked,
By the sweat and blood of his hand.

He is the one who should be thanked,
But he is given another cross to bear.
He will pay taxes from money earned.
What he makes he will have to share.

It may be too late for this to be fixed.
America has fallen too deep in debt.
Whoever wins it will be his task,
To make sure his promises are kept.

Only under God can our America survive.
Prayer will be our only answer today.
We must put our trust and hope in Him.
In my heart I know, there is no other way.

A WEDDING PRAYER

As you begin this new life together,
A wonderful event has occurred today.
It is a time to be remembered forever,
Every morning will bring a happier day.

Now as you begin this new life together,
Sweet moments will come along the way.
Know that the Lord will always be with you,
And now love's sweet light is here to stay.

Now as you begin this new life together,
You will not make earthly decisions alone.
You have a caring shoulder to lean on.
You have chosen each other to be that one.

Now as you begin this new life together,
You will not question this time or place.
God with infinite care brought you here.
And today, there is a smile on His face.

Now as you begin this new life together,
The prayer of your loved ones is the same.
That you enjoy your love and your new life.
And let this prayer be said in Jesus' name.

FALLEN HEROES

MEMORIAL DAY

I spent today with friends of mine,
In a peaceful atmosphere.
But then I thought of other things,
That happened throughout the years.

We did the normal things you do,
To celebrate this day.
There were some who were not there,
Who over the years fell by the way.

Their memory will not be dimmed by years,
Of how they lived and what they gave.
But it is not my plan to shed more tears,
Comfort is not found at stone or grave.

When you can remember how they lived,
And how they changed your world.
Or what they gave so you would be free,
Your joy should be to see that it is told.

If you are my family, then you too will miss,
Of who I speak and what they gave.
If you are not, then please remember this,
I am proud and Our God holds them safe.

Jean Carley

HERITAGE

For days on end I have tried to write,
A thought or message about this day.
It has been hard to find the words,
To let you know what I needed to say.

You see it has a special meaning for me.
I am so very proud of where I live.
I am an American, and I am free,
To worship God and allegiance give.

This country was formed by men of God,
Who in infinite wisdom answered a call.
So this country could thrive and grow,
And be a home for the great and small.

This is a great country, there is no doubt.
She is not perfect and things need to be done.
But never give up, you must never forget,
Those who faced the foe and the battle won.

Some gave their life, a country was born.
Others had no choice but to onward go.
They had come too far to ever turn back.
Today we should tell so all would know.

Pray for our country, each of you
That God will forever keep her free.
That she will always have a place of honor.
For you and I and the entire world to see.

REMEMBER THIS DAY

Perhaps there is a message somewhere,
So God can tell us how to handle this day.
So much has happened to our country this year.
Hearts are breaking; we are losing our way.

Celebrate by remembering the fallen ones.
Those on foreign soil and ones close by.
The young who had not yet lived their life.
It will not be our place to know the reason why.

We should pray for our country every day,
That America will be a home for the free.
And the lives that were lost to keep her safe,
Will always be remembered by you and me.

Do not ever take your freedom for granted.
If you do not take care, it may be lost.
It will only be guarded each and every day.
By those who are willing to pay the cost.

PAIN AND PEACE

POLICEMAN'S FUNERAL

I spent the morning watching a funeral,
That literally cut my heart to the core.
There is no way to escape my memories,
For they will be with me forevermore.

I have been where these mourners are.
I have known the searing pain they feel.
But I know there is the true assurance.
Our Lord gives strength for them to heal.

It takes a special breed to be the very best
There are not many that can attain.
The calling that God above must know,
Who ultimately make sacrifice their gain.

It will not be an easy road to travel.
There will be many days of unending grief.
Then one day the sun will seem brighter.
Peace will be found because of your belief.

Take comfort in knowing that above all.
This was a part of God's divine plan.
No one here knows the reason why.
You are not required to understand.

Jean Carley

THE HEROES OF THE COLE

Greatness, appreciation, then emptiness, sadness.
These were the things our leaders had to say,
Of those who paid the ultimate price with life.
We lost a part of America on that fateful day.

There is no way to describe the personal pain,
That every American has felt today.
There is no way to comfort the hurting families,
Who may never be able to let the hurt go away.

Then there are the ones who were left behind,
Who in fear and agony had to save their own.
In the confusion their bravery would rise.
They would have courage they had never known.

The injured who will suffer lifelong pain and grief.
But in God's plan, they were chosen to survive.
Yet they will remember the faces of their friends,
Who in their hearts and minds will still be alive.

Whoever these evil cowards may have been,
Who took the young lives of those we love.
Should realize they may have taken them from us.
But now they are with our Heavenly Father above.

THE HONOR OF AMERICA

Yesterday was the day set aside to honor,
All of those we have lost along the way.
In some way to remember the lives they gave,
So we could enjoy the life we live today.

In just about every heart there is an empty place,
Because someone was brave enough to die.
Maybe it was a friend or one of your family,
Who chose to answer a call and not ask why.

We have lost many young men and women.
Just this year as they served our country with pride.
In the danger of a foreign land to keep the peace.
In solemn awe with heartbreaking pain we cried.

Do not grow tired of speaking their praises.
It will be the least that you can do.
In some small way to honor their memory.
To repay them for what they did for you.

But that is the way it is for Americans you see.
Someone still has to do what our people do.
Pray for protection from our Heavenly Father.
You will have no choice; it is required of you.

REMEMBRANCE OF NINE-ELEVEN

Today I needed to write about Memorial Day,
A way to remember those we have lost.
The ones who protected our country knowing,
That they just might pay the ultimate cost.

A policeman willing to put his life on the line,
Just doing the job he always wanted to.
Never knowing when he answered the call,
That it would be required in service for you.

When times are quiet we can remember,
That someone we were blessed to meet.
The children we lost who will never know,
What life could have held for them to be.

Those who will not be here to grow old with us,
But the memories we have are sweet.
Keep this in mind as you pray for peace.
They gave their lives to protect you and me.

That is the way we are to remember them,
Because they are now in God's loving fold.
The blessings we gained by knowing them,
A place in our heart is a memory to hold.

TERROR ON NINE ELEVEN

Just the other day our pastor spoke,
Of a time in the life of everyone.
When they think that God has left them,
As if for something they may have done.

Do not ever doubt it, He is there with them.
They need only to reach for His hand.
He will hold them secure and love them
And with our America He will stand.

They must find comfort in His word.
They must be on their knees in prayer.
No other way can they ever survive.
They must rely on God's almighty power.

That's all they will have in days to come,
As they pick up the pieces of their lives.
We can only watch in stinging terror,
Allowing the tears to flow from our eyes.

So we pray to God, come near and comfort.
Give us peace of heart that only You can do.
We may be hurt, but we will never be down.
America's recovery will be a testament to You.

THE EAGLE CRIES

9-11

Today I saw the picture of an eagle,
With head bowed and a tear in its eye.
When I looked to my heart for an answer,
I came up with nothing other than why?

In his shadow was the Statue of Liberty,
And the twin towers that are no more.
They have been violently taken from us.
Be assured our leaders can even the score.

The innocent victims who did not know,
What was happening to them that day.
Most did not have time to say good-bye,
With scarcely time enough to pray.

But the living now has a daunting task,
To go on without the brave and best.
God will give the comfort that we need.
The world watches as we meet the test.

Do not doubt the strength of the eagle.
His feathers may be tattered and torn.
But he will not lose his cause to fly.
Out of this a new America can be born.

AMERICA THE PEOPLE

America has had to learn a lot of late.
She can be strong if she needs to be.
She can get up and dust herself off,
With pride for the entire world to see.

She can bury her dead with dignity,
And tell of courage on a written page.
If not for the brave, where would she be?
Their memories help to calm her rage.

Our God has not left us here alone.
He is holding us up as we find our way.
He was here with us in days gone by.
He will still be with us for each new day.

We must pray for our sons and daughters,
Who now fight in an evil and foreign land.
They hold high the banner of our freedom,
In the caring shadow of our Father's hand.

America was formed by men of God,
Who gave their lives so we could be free.
They did not have the luxury of an option.
The world watches you, what will it see?

THE POPPY IS OUT AGAIN

It comes around about this time every year.
The little red flower to wear on your lapel.
There's a lot of good in that little flower.
Veterans who sell them have a story to tell.

In some small way to help ease the pain,
Of a memory in their mind forever burned.
It's not something we have not heard before.
A loved one went to war and never returned.

Now we find our country at war once more,
And as always it is a fight we cannot lose.
There are sons and daughters far from home,
Sent to fight a war they did not choose.

We must support them with pride and prayer.
They went quickly without a backward glance.
Knowing full well they might not return.
For love of country, they will take this chance.

There were those in my family who served.
But they were returned to me safe and sound.
We must forever pray to our Heavenly Father.
Only in Him will lasting peace ever be found.

REMEMBRANCE

MEMORIAL AT GROUND ZERO

This has been a somber day of remembrance.
So many sad memories were brought to mind.
Of those whose lives were lost in brave actions,
After a year, for no good reason that we can find.

There is grief to be found on so many faces,
That perhaps nothing will ever take away.
So many innocent people who were taken,
Who with loved ones will not share another day.

The flowers silently placed with love in a crater,
In memory of some who may never be found.
And of those who were buried with honor,
In what will be considered hallowed ground

From a lonely farmer's field in Pennsylvania,
We can draw strength that only comes from God
To a building that is an emblem of our freedom,
Where patriots who on fields of battle have trod.

Never shall we ever allow our hearts to forget,
That we only find true comfort when we share.
That our Father is still in control of this world,
Without any doubt we know that He will care.

MEMORIAM FOR A POLICEMAN

Even a national tragedy did not
take you from my mind.
My prayers and thoughts were
with you all day through.
Even when the time I knew the cer-
emonies were to start,
And how what was to hap-
pen would have its effect on you.

The piercing shots that would make
your very soul shudder.
The playing of the melody that
would cut to your very heart.
The quiet after the ceremony was
over and you turned to leave.
This place you can return to, but
never find the missing part.

The different ways that man's respect
would be paid to him,
For the life he had lived and the profession he chose.
How his friends and compan-
ions would gather around you.
I am one who has been there and
can say that I also know.

I can tell you that with time your
heart will find its peace.
You will find your mind's own pri-
vate way to remember him.
His visions and deeds sustain you
and give you sweet comfort.
There are friends and family who
will always remember them.

He held a position that some can only dream to attain.
And now he is where it is quiet, peace-
ful and he is secure.
Your memories of him will live in your heart forever.
Love only the two of you could
share, forever will endure.

STORM AT THE UNKNOWN

They had been told they could stand-down.
They did not have to endure the storm.
They could return after it was over,
And everything had returned to norm.

It was not even up for discussion.
There was no decision for them to make.
They would stand united together,
To complete the task they chose to take

They stood on the post through the night,
To honor one who had died for us all.
The wind and the rain did not prevail.
Proud men who answered America's call.

The one they guarded is forever unknown.
He represents those who will never return.
And for the ones who today we may lose in battle,
A memory in our heart should forever burn.

I am so proud to be an American.
These men are an example of our very best.
The honor and privilege they stand for,
Has again proudly endured the test.

THOSE WHO DON'T RETURN

What can you say that has not been said before?
There is no new way to remember the loss.
Each individual has their own living memories,
Of someone whose life paid the ultimate cost.

I have lost no brother, father, or son in battle.
Although they each served their country well.
God has kept me and mine in His loving fold.
They each came home with stories to tell.

They knew what it was like to lose a friend.
They held the hands of grieving loved ones.
They handed the flag to wives and children,
And comforted mothers who lost their sons.

Many a soldier has never returned to loved ones.
And I have attended the funerals of some I knew.
This sort of thing burns a mark on your mind.
Somehow the ceremony always stays with you.

I know there is no comfort in grave or stone.
And your mind is a place where memories abide.
Your comfort has to be found in word and deed.
In the Heavenly Father a wounded spirit can hide.

Thank God for what you have and what it means.
To be an American and Honor them this way.
They died for you and never regretted the call.
Always find a place in your heart on this day.

UNITED STATES OF AMERICA

Today I'm going to reflect on America,
And the sad state of affairs that exists today.
If our founding fathers could see us now,
They would be shocked at how we lost our way.

We only see the words "In God We Trust,"
Because they are cut in marble on a wall.
We have even taken Him from our schools.
If we continue this way our nation will fall.

We allow our flag to be burned at the stake.
This is freedom of speech they tell me.
That flag stands for every freedom we have.
Without it I do not know where we would be.

It has flown above us in wars on foreign soils.
That were fought so you and I could be free.
It will always fly in my yard I am proud to say
Over one for the US Navy for everyone to see.

I will continue to honor my God and country.
I will celebrate the Fourth of July on this day.
I will pray she finds her way in this world.
I pray each day that God will show the way.

THE TEARS OF MEMORY

I hope you had a sad memorial day.
Maybe you might have even shed a tear.
As you remembered all we have lost.
Maybe even someone you held dear.

Maybe you even saw a lowered flag.
As you paid honor to those who died.
Or held the hand of an orphaned child,
And comforted a spouse as she cried.

I write this as our flag is brought to staff,
From eight o'clock until noon today.
So all may see that I have remembered,
Those who fell in a land so far away.

Again our soldiers fight on evil ground.
Many will return never to be the same.
They have seen a world we can only imagine.
Fears and nightmares only our God can tame.

The message I bring is different than most.
But what I write is straight from my soul.
God will cradle the lost in his loving fold.
Now to care for the living should be our goal.

Honor all of them as only we can, forever.

WOUNDED AMERICA

We are truly stunned beyond belief.
How on earth could this happen here?
How will our soldiers ever survive?
Now at home they must deal with fear.

God please take care of the wounded.
And welcome all those we have lost.
Please hold their families in your hand.
They have truly paid the ultimate cost

Those left will never lose their objective.
They will go onward with courage and pride.
They will hold memories in their hearts,
While tears of sorrow they cannot hide.

America, go to your knees in prayer today.
God give them strength to bury their dead.
They have done it many times before.
They will make us proud in days ahead.

Many flags will be folded in days to come.
Many of us have seen it close at hand.
Taps will sound and gunfire will echo,
And in all this the brave will still stand.

America was wounded at Ft. Hood,
But she will survive and can move on.
That is what we do in this country,
But the memories will never be gone.

NINE FROM NINE ELEVEN

How can we remember this time?
I hope a lot better than recent days.
There are those who seek to use it,
To get attention in dark and evil ways.

Not once do they mention those we lost,
They incite hatred for their fellow man.
We can still worship the way we choose.
Men and women gave their lives so we can.

Better we should try to move onward.
Our memories will always be close by.
Now we need to get our country back.
If we don't, this will surely be why.

We cannot let evil cloud our memory.
Everyone lost something on that day.
But we still have the right to worship,
In our own time and place, we can pray.

I will spend this day in quiet reflection,
And ask for guidance from God above.
That somehow He will see fit to give us,
The ability to touch others with His love.

JUSTICE FOR NINE ELEVEN

From the beginning we felt he should die.
There are times when you have no choice.
This was one time justice had to be done,
We had to employ an angry, violent voice.

Don't judge America unless you were there,
And watched as the Twin Towers would fall.
The ones who went into the flaming buildings,
Doing the duty to which they were called.

Hearts would break as we heard the stories,
Of family members who will never be found.
The husbands, wives, brothers, and sisters;
Now have met again on hallowed ground.

This war is not over and just may never be,
America does not give up without a fight.
We will continue to be proud of brave men,
Those who answer a call in the dark of night.

If there is to be satisfaction it must be ours.
We are the ones who have suffered the most.
We are the ones whose bravery will show.
We are the ones who have silenced the ghost.

FAMILY

SOMEONE SPECIAL

Someone special.
Who waits for me, patiently, lovingly.
Who really cares and lets me know it.

Someone special.
Who is considerate, compassionate,
And thoughtful.

Someone special
Always willing to help anyone,
Anytime any way.

Someone special
One of the Lord's workers, in his own way,
When it needs to get done.

Someone special
Can be depended on, works for the
Pleasure of seeing it done.

Someone special
I know one of these people; I live under his care.
I love him deeply, he is my husband.
I am blessed.

MY ROOTS

My roots are embedded deep in America.
From the mountains near Asheville,
To the tobacco fields of Lynchburg.
I am Virginia born.

My roots.
Were formed by the love of great parents.
Hard working who overcame obstacles, Who
overcame obstacles through hard work
For the good of their children.
No questions asked.

My roots
Shared with a brother and sisters.
Who looked over me,
With a deep-abiding love.
We still need each other.

My roots.
Will be carried on by my daughter,
Who is proud of her heritage.
Who knows and tells it with pride.
Who does ask questions.

My roots.
Sustaining, warm, wonderful, peaceful.
Blessed by our Lord.
Every American should be so lucky.
Grateful? Yes I am, every day!

CADBURY EGGS

Cadbury eggs almost look like the real thing.
Except they are wrapped in chocolate and foil.
Gooey inside, with a yellow yoke, all sweet and sticky.

Cadbury eggs, the favorite candy
for a young lady I know.
Her father knows this, and he never forgets.
Along about this time every year he buys them.

Cadbury eggs, sitting on my coun-
ter, waiting to be mailed.
Hunting for the right size box and the paper to wrap.
Figuring out which day they will be sent.

Cadbury eggs on the counter remind-
ing you of someone.
Every time you see them,
You wonder what she will think. What
is she doing, Where is she?
What will she remember when she gets them?

Cadbury eggs always sent to a daugh-
ter from her father.
Will she ever be too old for this ritual?
I kind of doubt it, but I am only her mother.

Cadbury eggs are one of my little memories,
Renewed this time every year.
Somehow she will always be our little girl.

I can see her now, eating the Cadbury eggs.
Trying not to get them on her
clothes or all over her face.
She is like that, our daughter, eating her Cadbury eggs.

SOMETIMES

Sometimes, I think of you for no reason,
Other than I love you.

Sometimes, I think of you for no reason,
Other than I miss you.

Sometimes, I think of you simply to wonder,
Where you are and what you are doing.

Sometimes, I remember what it was like,
When you were much younger.

Sometimes I think of times when
there was just the two of us,
Not knowing the future.

Sometimes, I had to make decisions you did not like,
because I could not help it.

Sometimes, times were good and I remember them,
Like the trip to Luray, just you, I, and Mandy.

Sometimes I think of times when
there was just the two of us,
Not knowing the future.

Sometimes I think of times when
there was just the two of us,
like when we went shopping for your birthday,
To get your ears pierced.

Sometimes there was just the two of us
But now you had a new father

Sometimes, your father who really loved
you took responsibility for you,
Who really loves you.

Sometimes, we simply could not agree on your friends,
I still loved you.

Sometimes, I am amazed at how close we are,
And how much we love each other.

Always remember it was worth it, and
I would do it all over again,
Maybe differently, maybe not.
This relationship of a mother and daughter.

A YOUNG MAN'S LIFE

A POLICEMAN

In the beginning, he was the joy of our family.
The third in a line of four.
The only boy in another generation.

In the beginning, he was a happy little boy,
Waiting for his only uncle.
To come by for a visit in the drink truck.

In the beginning, he started to grow up.
He became the man of the family.
Much too soon, but he would do well.

Then he became a man, doing most things early in life.
He made his mistakes, put them
behind him, moved on.
He became the man of the family, the big brother.

He became the husband to a wonderful young woman.
He became her child's father.
A credit to his community.

He held a job of high esteem,
Loved and respected by family and friends.
An example of all a man should be.

In the end, he rose high above the call of duty.
He answered the call with courage and pride.
He left us much too soon, so alone on a dark night.

In the end, we have memories that are not enough.
They will never be, but we will make do.
We must make him proud; I am sure he is watching.

OUR SON

He was a little boy once.
Long before I knew him.
I am sure he ran and played,
And did little boy things.

I met him later, when he was older.
A teenager, the toughest time.
At first he did not want me there,
But in time he came around.

He only had to learn he was loved.
We enjoyed special times.
He thought he was in control.
We planned it that way.

The he grew up, quickly! Overnight!
He was a young man.
Off to the navy he went.
I advised he not try to change them.

He came home with his crow, we were proud.
He dared his dad to wear his old uniform,
And they stood together.
His dad just did not breathe.
I know, I took pictures of the two.

Then he was off to change the world.
We gave advice, he listened, and he did,
Not always what was best,
But then he had to learn.

He came home to regroup, to open arms.
He had learned a lot, our son.
He could put his arms around us freely.
He could say how much he loved us.

He is out there now, where we cannot touch him.
Too far away, but with us in his spirit.
We are a family, and he is a part.
We are so lucky, his dad and I to have this son.

A GENTLE MAN

He is strong of stature.
He is honest and compassionate.
He is dignity personified.
He is a pillar of the community.

He is a father, husband, and man in the church.
He is a witness to all who know him.
He is pleasant, always polite.
He is expressed love from the heart.

He has lived a good life.
He is at peace with God and man.
He will well aware of life around him.
He is waiting for the Lord to take him home.

He will be so missed by so many.
He will expect us to let him go in peace.
He will not want us to cry.
He will want us to celebrate his life.

For my friend we will do this.
We have no choice.
It is determined by our Lord.
This is how it should be.

A FATHER

My father was a gentle man.
He possessed unmeasured love.
For each and every one he knew,
He expected the same of me.

My father was a gentle man
He was not ashamed to show emotion.
He had respect from all who knew him.
He expected the same of me.

My father was a gentle man.
All the children were his own.
He treated them equally with loving care.
He expected the same of me.

My father was a gentle man.
All his life he led his children,
With love, respect, and honor.
He expected the same of me.

My father was a gentle man.
In my eyes he could do no wrong.
He had a deep-abiding faith in God
He expected the same of me.

My father was a gentle man.
Only once did I see him anger.
He often bent his knee in prayer
He expected the same of me.

My father was a gentle man.
His handshake was his promise.
The look in his eyes sealed the bond.
He expected the same of me.

My father was a gentle man.
His obligation to his wife completed.
He quietly slipped away one night.
He is with her and the Lord.

At times when my memory wanders,
I think of how he might handle life.
I will do the best I can in his memory.
He would be gently pleased.

THE COMPLETED WALK

A MOTHER

She has completed what she was sent to do.
She did it well, and she will be blessed.
You should not question His judgment.
The Lord has taken her home to rest.

She is where it is quiet and peaceful.
His light will forever shine on her face.
And she will be waiting for each of you,
To join her in this wonderful place

Comfort and hold up each other now.
Ask for the Lord's leadership and care.
He will not fail you in your time of need.
Just call on his name and find Him there.

You will go onward, strong and at peace.
An example of God's love for each of you.
This is what she would have wanted.
Then you will be holding her memory true.

TO HONOR A MOTHER

A good mother is not too hard to find.
Just take a look around where you are.
More than likely there is one close by.
Giving out a special kind of love and care

Mothers, they come in all different sizes,
And from all the corners of the earth.
Just concentrate on the one you have,
Who's loved and prayed for you since birth.

She doesn't ever seem to be too tired,
From the everyday things she has to do.
To take the extra time to let you know,
She has a special love just for you.

Respect and honor must be given her.
It is decreed to you by God's command.
It will be a daily prayer from her heart,
That you are safe and secure in His hand.

As you step out to take you place in life,
And your mother's pride is showing through.
A loving smile, which is meant just for her,
Will be worth all the tears she shed for you.

MY CHILDREN

My children will not be with me on this day
They are all scattered here and there.
They are each in their own place to be.
They will call and I will know they care.

I can be at peace on Mother's Day.
I will know I have done the best I can.
And they will have their lives in order.
Yet I still pray they live according to His plan.

We have an abiding love for each other.
It will certainly span the years of time.
Knowing that when we visit with them.
Happiness in each other we will find.

God has promised He will take care of them.
They will never be far from his fold.
I find comfort in my faith and His grace.
It will always be there for me to hold.

If you have your children near with you.
You are blessed, this you should know.
Take advantage of all the years you have.
The time will come when they will go.

Just have a safe harbor they can come to,
When the world treats them unkind/
A loving embrace will make it right,
And then peace and comfort they will find.

Parents can do this; God helps.

VISITING ANGELS

"LOSS OF A CHILD"

Angels seldom come to earth,
But when they do, we know.
There's always something special.
That will be taught before they go.

Angels seldom come to earth.
Then they are only sent by the Lord.
He has something special in mind.
Sometimes only taught in his Word.

Angels seldom come to earth.
They only stay in special places.
Only trusted to certain people,
Who abide within God's graces.

Angels seldom come to earth.
They are only ours to borrow.
What we do while they are here,
Will ease our pain and sorrow.

Angels seldom come to earth.
God watches over them every day.
If you were chosen to care for one,
You were blessed in a special way.

Angels seldom stay on the earth.
They have a better place to be,
But we are better because of them.
In our Lord they will be forever free.

MOM'S FLYING NEEDLES

(DEDICATED TO A GRACIOUS LADY)
(FROM HER SON'S WIFE)

The needles do not knit anymore.
I cannot see the flying fingers.
But then I still have the bedspreads,
And other gifts of your love lingers.

The needles do not knit anymore,
But the light in your eyes still shine.
You have not lost your zest for life,
And wonderful memories are mine.

The needles do not knit anymore,
But you still have some work to do.
God is not through with you yet.
He still has tasks made just for you.

The needles do not knit anymore,
But the sweet spirit is still living there.
You have so much kindness yet to give.
Knowledge and experiences to share.

The needles do not knit anymore,
And that is certainly my loss to bear.
But you are with me in your spirit.
Look in your heart and find me there.

MOTHERS AND CHILDREN

This year Mother's Day will be special.
My children are safe and sound.
Although they are not here with me,
Love and memories with me are found.

God keeps them safe each and every day.
Because as a mother you ask Him to.
You know that He will never let them go.
And will be there to see them through.

Children,

Go to your mother today and thank her.
Get in touch with her however you may.
Let her know how much you love her.
Let her know you think of her every day.

There is nothing you can give to her,
That will ever mean quite as much.
As a special look known only to her.
Or love shown by your special touch.

Jean Carley

LEGACY OF A FATHER

Trying to write a message about a father,
Is not a very easy thing to do.
It will always be a very personal thing,
That is found in the heart of each of you.

There will be memories that you hold dear,
When things of the world break your heart.
And he is always there to make it better,
Standing beside your mother to do his part.

He makes your home feel safe and secure.
A place you can always come back to.
You are never too old to be his child.
He holds a place in his heart just for you.

If you are blessed to have him with you,
Never forget what he does every day.
He will never tire of caring for you.
He just wants to be there to show the way.

No matter what this life has dealt you,
It is much like our Heavenly Father above.
Who will always offer his hand to lead you,
And keep you safe with His unending love.

CALL WAITING

MOTHER AND DAUGHTER

I sit here and wait for her to call me.
Not knowing how things are with her.
I have to go with no news is good,
Until I can hear that things are better.

I have to learn to be patient now,
And let her handle things on her own.
She knows what she has to do,
Until the final outcome is known.

In all instances I am her mother,
And this will always be the case.
I will not be at peace with this,
Until I can see her face-to-face.

Give us wisdom we need to help her.
Tell us what to do and what to say.
So she can make decisions on her own,
And peace comes in the Lord's way.

SOUTH DAKOTA SNOW

A card came today from my brother.
He and his are traveling out west.
He and his wife are traveling out west
They are where I want soon to be.
They say this time of life is the best.

They showed pictures of mountains,
And talked of snow in South Dakota.
They just moved a bit farther south.
To them right now, time has no quota.

They said they wished we were there,
Sharing this time would be so right.
We have started making travel plans.
We looked at books and maps last night.

Each day now we think of something,
That must be done before we can go.
When the time comes we will be ready.
Where we will stop, we still don't know.

Anticipation makes our hearts beat faster.
We don't know when we will be back.
But I bet you the first thing we will do.
Is sit down and tell it all to my brother, Jack.

So I must now pray for His comfort.
He knows what will come about.
Let Him put us all under angel wings,
And protect us from worry and doubt.

THIS BABY-A GIFT

God has sent you a special little angel,
Created by your love for each other.
There is no greater calling on this earth,
Than the privilege of being a mother.

God has sent you a special little angel.
Now your life will never be the same.
You have answered to another calling.
Guidance will come, just ask in His name.

God has sent you a special little angel.
And He is giving you the time to prepare,
For the life you have brought to this world,
And the duty the two of you will share.

God has sent you a special little angel.
And for both of you our prayers are one.
Look forward to this time of your life.
And let the Lord be the head of your home.

BIRTHDAYS

"TEENAGER BIRTHDAY"

Life is moving so fast for you right now.
Wonderful things are happening every day.
This birthday will be one of those memories.
It will stay with you as you make your way.

Looking back on life helps find the future,
And where you are and what you should do.
Always guard your outlook on this life.
It helps to find the pathway best for you.

Accept true friendship when it is offered.
Learn how to accept advice from those,
Who have been where you will be going.
Taking responsibility for the life you chose.

Making decisions will give you satisfaction.
Always be willing to learn from your mistakes.
Then you can accept all the wonderful rewards,
That hard work and accomplishment makes.

There are those who love and care for you.
They have given to you from their very souls.
Make sure you never forget who they are.
Because of them you will reach your goals.

Jean Carley

GOOD DAY'S VISIT

We waited for the day to come,
When you would finally be here.
We knew before it was over,
We both would shed a tear.

We knew we couldn't do it all,
There would be things left to say.
But we will still take care of it.
It will just have to be another day.

We cannot allow any options.
It is something that must be done.
We must work on it together.
The task cannot fall to just one.

There are those who do not care,
Don't allow it to change our mind.
A peace and comfort we will know.
They will not be able to find.

Show them how our hearts smile.
How the sun shines on our faces.
And in the end we will be secure.
Our memories dwell in peaceful places.

CLOSE BY

I've never been too far away from you.
You've always known how to find me.
It's just that the time had to be right,
And the opportunity there for us to see.

If you needed, I would have been there,
Of that there is no doubt in my mind.
I would have come to you in a heartbeat.
If peace or comfort I could help you find.

You see that is what families are for.
To nourish and comfort each other.
It was not meant that we have options.
We just need to take care of one another.

There is comfort in how it came to be.
That God brought you here for a day.
We got so much accomplished you see.
Just being together in our private way.

Don't ever think you are far from me.
You are in my heart in a special place.
We don't always need to talk in words.
I can just think of you and see your face.

WRITTEN MEMORIES

MOTHER-IN-LAW

I write this in memory of one I have loved,
    Who filled a spot in my worldly walk.
One who I could always count on to be there,
    Because sometimes I just needed to talk.

I write this in memory of one I remember,
    Who kept the hearth warm on a winter day.
Who for a while in her life shared our home,
    When I was younger and finding my way.

I write this in memory of a caring mother,
    Who had only a few earthly riches she shared.
But who stood by her children all her life,
    Proud of each of them, she always cared.

I write this in memory of a loving friend,
    Who got up each day and lived her life.
She made the best of what she was dealt.
She found no fault with this world's strife.

I write this in memory of one of another faith,
    Who supported me completely in mine.
Who prayed for a son to find his salvation,
No matter it was a faith of a different kind.

WHAT FRIENDS DO

A NEIGHBOR'S SUICIDE

We are here for you when you just want to talk,
About this terrible pain that life has dealt.
We would not ever say we know how you feel,
The awesome hurt you know we have not felt.

But we know that our God does care for you.
We are praying he will make his presence known,
In ways that will give you comfort and peace.
If you just wait on Him, it will surely be shown.

Try and find sweet times to remember the good.
Hold on to each other when you talk or just cry.
Do not try to think of what you might have done.
It could be you might never know the reason why.

The path between our houses is there for a reason.
Walk it any time your heart feels the need.
And know that no matter what time of night or day,
There is love and compassion on which you can feed.

Your friends will gather around to comfort you.
They will always be standing just outside your gate.
Just to help you put the pieces back together.
Take your time; things of this world can wait.

LOVE IN A WORD

GRANDDAUGHTER

This is a special day you may never forget.
It was when a wonderful thing occurred.
You will tell her about it from time to time.
The day she surprised you with her first word.

You were not prepared to hear her say it.
It's not what you thought it would be.
Maybe some other word you often repeated,
Or something that every day she could see.

But you will soon learn how it is with children.
They do not do things as you want them to.
Their opinion of how important things are to be,
Most of the time is totally foreign to you.

I am sure you have often whispered to her,
How you are overwhelmed by her charms.
Just how glad you are God gave her to you,
When she peacefully sleeps in your arms.

There will be many more times of first things.
The first step and all the things little girls do.
But just right now on this particular day,
It was important that she said the word love to you.

GREEN MEMORY

I always knew it was somewhere,
I had seen it in times before.
A beautiful green with other colors.
Another like it would be no more.

It was something special made with love.
It was one of a kind meant just for me.
With every stitch needed to make it complete,
So when I was older her love I would see.

Over the years I thought it had gone astray.
That someone had it who did not know.
That this had been made just for me to have.
I always knew in my heart that it would show.

It was meant to carry on a tradition of love.
She had three grandchildren, and I was one.
Something I could always remember her by.
And I could pass it on to a daughter or son.

The quilt has now come to rest with me.
For years it was with a member of the family.
When they were reminded of what I knew,
It was placed where it was meant to be

IN MEMORY

Somehow before I was told I knew,
That my friend was no longer here.
That he had gone to be with his Father,
And knowing him, there was no fear.

The journey has now been completed.
He has done what he was sent to do.
He did it well, and he will be blessed.
He was an example for each of you.

Now he is where it is serene and peaceful.
You see he just moved over to God's place.
There is no more suffering, and he is free.
God's peace and love shines from his face.

You should comfort and hold each other.
Ask for God's wonderful leadership and care.
He will not fail you in your time of need.
Just call on His name and find Him there.

You must go onward, strong and in peace.
That is what He would have wanted for you.
We are not to question our Father's decision.
Just rest in God and hold his memory true.

MORE THAN A DAY

I've often watched other grandparents,
As they proudly doted over a little one.
And wondered why they were so awed.
Now I find that is what I have become.

I so much wanted to simply hold her tight,
And let her go to sleep on my shoulder.
But that special time may have to wait,
Until this child gets to be a little older.

Because of what life has assigned us,
We find we are many miles from each other.
We do not see her as often as we would like.
I miss so much, being a distant grandmother.

When we met she did not quite remember me.
Maybe if I had just a little more than a day.

Then there would be a special spot for me,
She would know why things are this way.

But a day will come when she will know,
That although I do not live close by.
That I love her just as much in my heart,
And I have a place there, just for her and I.

EVERYDAY THINGS

There are lots of things we come across,
In our every day walk in this life.
Some are easy and some we find hard.
The aim must be, it not cause us strife.

There are things that will not change,
No matter how hard we may try.
Just look for the total picture to see,
And don't even try to know why.

There are two sides to every story.
The reason people do the things they do.
It may never change and that's okay.
Just don't let it get the better of you.

Like how he leaves the wet towel,
Laying out for me to put away.
He never closes the bathroom curtain,
And his shoes are always in the way.

I know that there will be many things,
That I find now I am glad to overlook.
You see I still have him with me.
We can write more pages in our book.

MOTHER'S BIBLE

Today I found a letter in Mother's Bible.
Written in my father's hand it told,
Of commitment and undying love.
Tattered and brown, sixty-six years old.

Things of importance were mentioned.
Of children and how they would be raised.
A home where love and respect would be.
In one paragraph God's name was praised.

He lost his wife and was a single father.
He cared for his girls; his love was known.
Family and friends gathered around him.
But at the end of the day, he was alone.

Her husband died and left her alone with two.
She worked all day to provide their care.
So young they did not remember their father.
But this man had enough love to share.

This letter tells of God's plan for two people.
Of a love that would span the years of time.
Two that God would use to form a union.
To make a family that I am proud is mine.

THEY WERE HERE

Today I looked at all my pictures,
Of children who live so far away.
I remembered our wonderful visit,
How I watched them run and play

I remember the bouncing ponytails,
Laughter, shy smiles, hugs, and kisses,
Games they played and stories told.
All these things my heart now misses.

Crawling on my bed to watch cartoons;
A private place for laughing and talking.
The joy of holding them tight and close;
A hand in mine when we were walking.

One whose heart is tender and sweet.
Looked in my eyes and said I love you.
I put my arms around and held her close.
My heart was stolen, what could I do?

I love the son and wife who shared them.
I'm sure I probably broke a rule or two.
But it is nothing they cannot correct.
This is just something grandparents do.

STRENGTH

MOTHER OF A DISABLED CHILD

With all that is in my heart, I stand in awe of you.
The strength you have could only be from God.
There is no way any other could know your pain,
Unless the path you walk they also have trod.

Yet I am sure there have been times in your life,
When the tears flowed and your heart did break.
Yet there was no outward sign you every faltered,
To make a life better was the path you chose to take.

I know in my heart God was with you every day.
That is what I prayed for when I thought of you.
That He would guard your life and give you hope,
And you would know how much He loved you.

He has made you an example to those around you,
On how to live their lives and put aside their fears.
Your family and I have learned from your presence,
And it is an honor to have you walk with us here.

This is a time in your life you will never forget.
The years you showed compassion, hope, and care.
You were the loving mother of a disabled child.
You did your job well; you have crowns to wear.

FAMILY

We waited for them as evening came.
Their visit we had looked forward to.
Now they were here safe and sound,
It is my joy to share this with you.

They brought pears from a tree in the yard.
They talked of things like an early frost,
And apples they picked and gave to me,
And green tomatoes so they won't be lost

Most of our time was spent with history.
Of a lifelong career of preaching the word.
Of raising children and building a home,
Of family and all the good things I've heard.

They talked of the mountains of Virginia,
And their serene beauty this time of year.
It reminded me of my life back there,
And all the memories I now hold dear.

My prayer will be their safe journey home,
And the chance to visit them next year.
They are family, the Reynolds blood.
Whatever God has in store, there is no fear.

FIELD OF SCENES

I found them outside a window.
It brought memories to my mind.
Of wonderful days that used to be.
It was a beautiful place to find.

Scenes of life came back as I saw it,
To make a living by tilling the land.
The work you do, the life you lead,
Being blessed by God's own hand.

A family pulls together every day,
What it takes to get the job done.
To be bone weary at end of the day,
But in your heart the battle's won.

To see the beauty of the green earth,
When a crop is safely stored away.
The animals will be fed that winter.
To be at peace at the end of the day.

This is a life that many do not know
Perhaps that is how it should be
So I can tell this story to those I love
I have been there; this is a joy for me.

ENVELOPE POWER

IN GOD WE TRUST

It has got to start somewhere,
So today I made the change.
It's a message I'll be sending,
A nice thing, not all that strange.

It will travel as far as I send it.
Be it a message or to pay a bill.
Now maybe others will do it now,
And it just might be God's will.

I feel good about what I'm doing.
It could have been done long ago.
I just needed a nudge from a friend,
Now pride in my country will show.

We have lost our way in America.
Courts have ruled away our right.
To show our motto to the entire world.
This way it is in everybody's sight.

All we have to do is trust in Him,
And let Him guide America's way.
It can be done; now it's up to us.
Put it on your mail; it's back to stay.

ASK ONLY ONCE

We only need to ask You once.
We know You'll do what's best.
Just give us the courage now,
That we need to stand this test.

Guide family as we help each other.
Be it to go or just wait by the side.
Prayers made will be answered.
Your face from us You do not hide.

No matter what the trial to come,
I have brothers and sisters with me.
The stand beside me in Your name.
Their presence and comfort we can see.

There is a brighter day waiting
As we walk in this valley of tears.
We know it will be there for us,
As it has been for all of our years.

We will feel Your very presence,
If the answer we do not understand.
You will still lead us as we go our way,
Sheltered in the palm of Your hand.

BACK HOME AGAIN

I went back to summit while I was there,
To a house where roots were put down.
It will never be the same as it used to be,
But a place where memories are found.

I went back to where my parents rest.
It will always have a place in my heart.
I went there when the world was cold,
Or if I needed a softer place to start.

I traveled the roads of years gone by.
They did not take me to familiar places.
The changes are too many to number.
There were no longer friendly faces.

But I will remember my journey back,
And I met with some I had known before.
I can remember things that used to be,
And it was good to see them once more.

I learned a pleasant lesson on this trip.
There will always be something to find.
So you know you can go home again,
And make memories of a different kind.

THE DOG TAG

He was respected by those he knew.
He lived a quiet life with his fellow man.
He never knew anything but hard work.
He lived his life by the turn of his hand.

He always had the respect of his children.
They understood by the look on his face.
That nothing was more important to him,
Than to be with them in that time and place.

These days generations span centuries.
He was born in eighteen ninety-three.
He never talked that much about this time,
But he still served so we would be free.

On this day I will wear his dog tag,
Given for the war of many years ago.
In this way I can honor my father,
For a time most people no longer know

GOD'S CREATURES

THERE IS THAT BIRD

That bird.
Hopping around in that cage, top to bottom.
Side to side, flapping wings, spraying seeds.

That bird.
Up on that perch like it owns this place,
Turning that blue head from side to side.

That bird.
A bird that mocks our dog, no way,
We have a bird like that, something else, that bird.

That bird.
Took a long trip with us, bouncing up the road.
His cage sitting on the floorboard of the truck.

That bird.
Who can say the words just like you?
When he wants to get your attention.

That bird.
As small as he is, can get your attention.
Make you talk to him when he chirps.

That bird.
Who mimics your voice on the phone machine?
People think we're home when we're not.

That bird
So much joy and sweetness,
In a small blue package.
Drawing us into his world on his terms.

That bird.
It didn't take long for him to get me trained.
Little blue birds named Tweety are like that.

A DOG

A dog is a special gift from God for man.
Always has been, always will be.
Unconditional love.

A dog is unconditional love expressed by
The look of love in their eyes for their masters.
A bright light.

A dog is a bright light at the end of a long day.
A wagging tail, happy bark demanding attention.
It's responsibility.

A dog is responsibility given to you by God.
After all it is one of his creatures, perfect.
A very special something.

A dog is something you must take care of,
In doing so you are given comfort.
A small need to be filled.

A dog does not need much, a bowl of water
A bowl of food, a loving pat, and a kind word.
Unquestioning trust.

A dog will always trust you when in need.
It will trust you with its life and give it for you.
What more can you ask.

A dog will never be understood, why or how it
Does things is a mystery shared only with God.
A dog, one of God's creatures,
Beautiful and needed.

MOTHER NATURE

Today I sit and look outside,
At the land behind my house.
It is a home to God's creatures,
From the eagle to the mouse.

It is peaceful out there today.
There is nothing to dismay.
They all get along together;
His creatures enjoying the day.

The cranes come for their dinner,
Put down by a caring brother.
The little ones tag along behind,
Keeping up is quite a bother.

The egrets perch upon a tree,
After walking stately for a time.
Watching for the water to move,
So their dinner they can find.

The squirrels come to the feeder,
That's an easy meal to find.
Ever with an eye to the house,
With a brown dog on their mind.

Quail scamper across the grass,
From one place to another.
They may stop under the feeder,
And call out to each other.

Even the black snake in the yard,
Is a welcome sight to see.
He keeps the bad ones away,
His way of protecting you and me.

CARDINAL COMFORT

LOSS OF A PET

After a year I thought it would be easier,
But I found some comfort just the other day.
When I saw a cardinal on a tree stump,
As if a message had been sent my way.

It told me that God takes care of the least.
That he knows of every hair and feather.
That although I still feel the pain of loss,
I know in my heart I want to be better.

No matter how it happened on that day,
My heart still carries a pain that will show.
God handled it in the way He knows best.
And I should let that be all I need to know.

You see my heart is tender by my nature.
That is the way that God meant me to be.
It has held me in good stead over the years.
It's been my witness for others to see.

His creature was given to me for a reason.
Maybe just to show how God wants us to be.
To love and care for the ones He gives us.
I pray now that my heart He will set free.

HOLIDAY
CELEBRATIONS

A SEASON OF RENEWAL

A season of renewal is Easter.
Life starts all over.
It did for Jesus.

A season of renewal is spring.
Things bloom all over.
Color abounds.

A season of renewal is hope.
No matter how sad you are,
Things will be better.

A season of renewal is kindness.
A touch of a hand, a smile,
It is always needed.

A season of renewal is love.
When generously given,
Awards the giver even more.

A season of renewal is caring.
Just being aware of another's pain,
And doing what has to be done.

A season of renewal is welcome.
Always finds an open door.
Just enter, enjoy, give thanks.

A season of renewal is faith.
When you have known all the above,
It will sustain and support you.

KIDS AND CHRISTMAS

It's been so great to have you here.
You have made our holiday,
Just by being here with us.
You were such a light along the way.

It's been so great to have you here,
To share your love and good cheer.
It has made Christmas what it is.
Without kids, holidays would be so drear.

It's been so great to have you here,
To see you grin from ear to ear.
To watch as you enjoyed your visit,
And know it was because you care.

It's been so great to have you here.
To know this is where you wanted to be.
Of all the places you could have gone,
You chose to be with your Dad & Me.

It's been so great to have you here.
We have made another happy time.
One that we will hold on to,
And make it last forever in our mind.

It's been so great to have you here.
When you get home safe and sound,
Although the trip will be long.
Just never forget where home is found.

RESOLUTIONS

Here we are again, and it's a brand new year.
We are healthy and happy with help from above.
The Lord has really been so good to us.
Everything that's happened is because of his love.

We have learned and accomplished a lot this year.
Happy that we have grown closer to our Lord.
The love of friends and family truly abounds,
After all, is this not just another great reward.

Resolutions made by man that are of his own needs,
Must be from guidance found only by God's grace.
Then we can only expect His very best to us.
And know that everything will find its place.

Most of all I would hope that you find true peace.
It is not his intent that your life be in turmoil.
Do not dwell on the bad and create more suffering.
What has happened is not of your control.

I would wish for all of you to simply stand and wait.
Everything that has happened is for a reason.
What is to happen is only known by God.
We must simply trust Him and rest for this season.

THANKS

Thanksgiving Day is here again,
And with it comes other things.
Like turkey, yams, and pumpkin pie.
And all the joy it brings.

Thanksgiving Day is here again.
With weather crisp and clear.
It is that time of year again,
When we start to feel good cheer.

Thanksgiving Day is here again.
There are a lot of things to do.
Remember why we celebrate,
And who we should give credit to.

Thanksgiving Day is here again,
Based on religious freedom sought.
All should know how we got started.
Remember the price of freedom bought.

Thanksgiving Day is here again.
Lift up your prayers to your Lord.
Be thankful it is here you live,
Sustained by the power of His word.

Thanksgiving Day is here again.
Join with me in offering praise,
To him who blesses us in every way,
And thank him for this holiday.

THE TRIP

The trip was long, and they were tired.
Her body ached with exhausting pain.
Choice was not theirs to make this time,
But this trip would not be made in vain.

It had been a long hard road to travel.
They prayed for the end of a very long day.
If they could only make it to their destination,
Where they could find a quiet place to stay.

As day turned to evening, they arrived,
But much later than they had thought.
When they tried to find a resting place,
There was not even one to be bought.

They were tired and did not have a choice.
And she would not have a comfortable bed.
But they would take shelter of any kind.
A place for Joseph's Mary to lay her head.

The next day the world was a different place.
For during this night Mary found no rest.
The world as they knew it changed forever.
What Mary wrapped from God was blessed.

His gift to the world. His name was Jesus.

THE CHRISTMAS CARDS

Guess what? My Christmas cards are done.
Must be I have the Spirit.
Never had them done this fast before.
I may get this mess in order yet.

Guess what? My Christmas cards are done.
I even have a few ideas on what to buy.
But I still have so much to do.
I can get this mess in order; I'll just try.

Guess what? My Christmas cards are done.
Now I'll find out who I forgot.
Will I have my house straight in time?
Or else my decorating will go to pot.

Guess what? My Christmas cards are done.
When I think of all I still have to do,
What I will do next is the question
That's always been my status quo.

Guess what? My Christmas cards are done.
Greetings sent to friends and family afar.
Now everything will happen in its time.
Family will arrive, the house will glow.

Guess what? My Christmas cards are done.
I just remembered what we often forget.
There is so much to be thankful for.
Like the birthday celebration soon to be.

Guess what? My Christmas cards are done.
Now all I have to do is get myself in line.
I only have to remember what it's all about.
This thing called Christmas, God's time.

Have a happy birthday, Lord,
My Christmas cards are done.

THE WEARING OF THE BELLS

Today I wore the Christmas bells,
To let everybody know I was here.
One was red and one was green,
Meant to ring in the Christmas cheer.

Today I wore the Christmas bells.
I baked cookies and bought candy,
Trying to get people around here happy.
Some Christmas spirit would be dandy.

Today I wore the Christmas bells.
I've been hanging cards on the wall.
I'm still walking around in stores,
But I've finished my shopping overall.

Today I wore the Christmas bells.
Maybe next week we'll get it together.
Forget bah-humbug and remember ho ho ho.
It would be easier if we had cold weather.

Today I wore the Christmas bells,
And this week our kids will come.
Bet you then everything will get better.
Because the spirit will be in my home.

HE IS NOT THERE

He is not there.
They have taken Him down from the cross.
He has been laid in a borrowed tomb.
If only we could see Him again.

But He is not there.
Thoughts of what they did when He was here,
Brings so much pain to our hearts.
If only we could see Him again.

But He is not there.
Even the tomb could not hold Him.
The emptiness that is felt by this world.
If only we could see Him again.

But He is not there.
He has left to be with His Father.
We have to wait for His return.
If only we could see Him again.

And He is there.
He told us He would prepare a place,
And then return to take us home.
If only we could see Him again.

But He never left us.
He walks with us every day.
Look upward to the heavens,
Because we will see Him again.

This is the hope of the world.

OUR CELEBRATION

It was such a wonderful service.
Each one did their part so well,
To bring everything together,
So His story we could tell.

From early in the morning,
Until the late part of the day.
We celebrated His resurrection.
Telling the steps along the way.

In the evening of this special day,
We went to our knees to pray.
In order to be at peace with Him.
The ending to His perfect day.

His supper we shared in honor.
This is what we are told to do.
Never to forget how much He gave.
And what He did for me and you.

Do not just remember this special time,
But rather take it with you every day.
And tell His story from your heart,
For if He lives there, He will show the way.

OVERSHADOWED

"BRUSH FIRE DESTRUCTION"

The Fourth of July will come and go,
Without its fanfare and celebration.
But this is one we will remember,
It has held our undivided attention.

There are those who lost everything.
All their earthly goods and wares.
But they must just remember this,
There is one who loves and cares.

To those who do not know Him,
He could sustain you in this trial.
You could recover with His help.
But even now there will be denial.

Those who have accepted his comfort,
Is an example of hope to everyone?
They move forward with His strength,
Knowing that they were never alone.

No matter what has happened to you,
It was always in His infinite control.
Good or bad He has taken care of you.
Thank him from the bottom of your soul.

THE CHRISTMAS CARD

When I sat down to write this letter,
The season was not yet here.
But the joy we know in our heart,
Should be felt all through the year.

God's blessings I would wish for you,
As we celebrate this time of year.
Remember why we have this season,
And you will feel His presence near.

Tell of the joy and peace in your heart.
Spread love and happiness as you go.
All because Mary's child was born,
And still lives today, His love to show.

TURKEY DAY

We will have a quiet turkey day this year.
Thanking the Lord for all He has given us.
We will sleep late and take life easy.
It will be our choice not to make a fuss.

The dinner I cook may be a bit special.
Just not the ordinary things we often fix.
Some dressing and gravy on our plates.
And tender turkey will likely do the trick.

I'll make a favorite cobbler just for us.
Just something that's not done every day.
Husband will then sleep through the game,
And I will occupy myself another way.

Actually I'm looking forward to the day.
Our kids will call with love and wishes.
I will let my day take my own good time.
I can even let the washer do the dishes.

This may not be the traditional way,
That one is to spend Thanksgiving Day.
But this is what we want to do.
Just whose business is it anyway?

I will not forget the Pilgrims' trip.
In You they placed their life and trust.
It is because of them we are blessed.
Thank you, Lord, for all you did for us.

AMERICA'S VETERANS

Today will be the day we can honor,
All the ones we lost along the way.
To remember them for what they gave,
To bring our country safely to this day.

Do not grow tired of speaking their praises.
It is to be the least that you can do.
In some small way to repay them,
For what they gave for each of you.

The Civil War fought here at home,
That brought our country to its knees.
The healing of the wounds that came,
When at last we found a blessed peace.

The First World War on foreign ground,
That took our fathers and sons away.
So many never came back home.
But they are at peace wherever they lay.

To all who have fought since that time,
We must honor them just the same.
Be proud that you are an American today,
So their lives were not laid down in vain.

Always hold in your heart a place of honor,
For those who answered our nation's call.
And in the end when the roll is to be called,
It will mean more than a name on a wall.

THE COMING YEAR

There are so many things that have happened,
To each of us throughout this year.
There was good and there has been the bad,
And through it all, He was always near.

We have all accomplished a lot this year,
Happy that we have grown closer to the Lord.
The love of friends and family holds us safe.
In our hearts, his can be just another reward.

We each have so much to look forward to,
As we welcome in another new year.
Things we should do to help each other,
As we trust in Him to make our pathway clear.

Resolutions made by man that are of his own needs,
Must be with the guidance found in God's grace.
Then we can expect His very best for each of us,
And know that everything will find its place.

Most of all it is His intent that we find true peace.
Everything that happens will be for a reason.
We must simply trust in Him to safely lead us,
To find happiness and comfort in this season.

HAPPY BIRTHDAY JESUS

Christmas Day will come and it will go,
After all it's just another birthday.
And they all somehow tend to hurry by,
With all the commercials that come our way.

But if in your heart you really love Him,
And know He came to give His life for you;
You have no choice but to honor Him.
Not just one day but the whole year through.

So find some quiet time meant just for Him,
And just tell Him how much you really care.
And then your holiday will be truly blessed,
And with Him this season you can share.

THE LILY

The Easter lily has not bloomed yet.
The symbol of His sacrifice and love.
It's just sitting there in my garden.
As if waiting for a sign from above.

There have been so many bad things,
That has happened to us this year.
Things that brought tears to our eyes,
And filled our hearts and souls with fear.

Could it be it is waiting for a better time
To open up and show us its pretty face?
Maybe to be a sign of peace and love,
That we so sorely need here in this place.

It is alive and simply waiting for its time.
Just like all of His beautiful things.
So pray for faith and understanding,
Then enjoy the comfort this always brings.

THE FOURTH OF NINETY-NINE

This Fourth of July will be so different,
Than the one we knew last year.
This year we will be able to celebrate,
With no fires to fill our hearts with fear.

As a country we have known a storm or two.
We have found an unwanted tear in our eye.
And some still have burdens on their hearts.
But our lot is not to know the reason why.

Remember why we have this holiday.
Try to do what we can do to make it right.
Pray earnestly for God's leadership and grace,
That we can go onward living in His light.

We must come together as a country,
And try to return to what we used to be.
Founded on Christian faith and honor,
So we will always be the land of the free.

Do not take those who died for granted.
Without them our freedom would be lost.
We must be willing to guard it every day,
By supporting those willing to pay the cost.

ALLEGIANCE

I pledge my allegiance to my America.
Our ancestors died so it could be free.
It was not as if there was ever a question.
When they were there, it was for you and me.

There are things wrong here in our country.
Our values and directions are not clear.
Nothing will be done if we leave it to others.
We are responsible for what happens here.

We have rights, which cannot be taken away,
To peacefully protest things that is wrong.
The right to vote and express our opinion.
The right to stand and sing America's song.

If all you do is wave the stars and stripes,
Do it with your pride and love on your face.
Let everyone know just how glad you are,
That you can live here because of God's grace.

A SEASON OF THANKS

Let's try to have a good Thanksgiving,
In spite of those we lost along the way.
It will never be our place to know why.
Just do your best to make it a better day.

Let's try to have a good Thanksgiving,
Though our hearts are heavy with pain,
For the bad things that happened this year.
Jesus will help us find His peace again.

Let's try to have a good Thanksgiving.
Remember the storms He led us through,
With His loving care and protection.
He made the pathway safe for each of you.

Let's try to have a good Thanksgiving.
He will always hear us when we pray.
Even when we stray outside the fold,
He brings us back and shows the way.

Let us gather with friends and family,
And thank the Lord for all He has done.
He is still taking care of us every day.
He has blessed us, each and every one.

We must now seek direction from our God.
He was invited when this country began.
We must not leave Him out of plans we make.
If anyone can help, I know that He can.

THE MESSAGE

I have to come up with something for Christmas.
Just a little message to send a warm greeting.
But try as I might I cannot find the words.
Perhaps the Lord and I should have a meeting.

There are always lots of things that I could say.
Trouble is somebody got there well before me.
Coming up with something with just my touch,
May not be what He wants the message to be.

When you get back to basics, you can get it done.
That is where I guess He wants me to go.
After all it comes down to the same old story.
How Jesus was born two thousand years ago.

Enjoy this time with family and your friends.
Use it as a time to remember the Blessed One.
Who came to us on a cold winter's night,
To change the world; His work is still not done.

BECAUSE IT'S CHRISTMAS

I sat down today to write about Christmas.
A time to celebrate the Master's birth.
When He was born in a lowly manger,
God's only begotten Son to live on earth.

His fate was decided before He was born.
He would live just more than thirty years.
But what would He be able to accomplish,
By the shedding of His blood and tears?

He would save your soul from eternal loss.
He would make a pathway just for you.
It would not be because you deserved it,
But because that is what He wanted to do.

Let this time be used to show His love,
To each and every life that you may touch.
This in some small way to try and repay Him,
Because only He could love you that much.

BUSY-BUSY

The first wave of the holidays is over.
We've eaten our turkey and pumpkin pie.
We now look forward to Christmas.
Then New Year's Day will be close by.

Today I will have to venture out to shop,
For something I just cannot do without.
Either this or my tree will be topless.
This cannot happen; there is no doubt.

I will soon have all my cards ready to go.
The outside of the house is all done.
Now soon I will start baking cookies.
If we could just have no calories in just one.

I still have my presents to buy and wrap.
Many important things yet to be done.
But everything will soon come together.
I will have done them, each and every one.

Greet people with loving smiles and hugs,
Always keep the spirit alive in your heart.
If you remember Christ was born on this day,
In the end you will have done your part.

HERE IT COMES

I have been so busy looking to retirement,
That Christmas got lost by the wayside.
And now here it is just a few days away,
And I wish I had a place to run to and hide.

I have gotten the important things done.
My letters are mailed and my writing done.
I have sent greeting to friends and family.
I just hope I did not forget anyone.

I've got most of my shopping yet to do.
I don't even know what I will buy.
But like years past it will come together.
Husband will help me to hang in there and try.

One set of kids will come to visit,
And we will have good times around the tree.
Dinner will be cooked, I did buy the ham.
My joy will be in the love shared with me.

The joy of Christmas should be told to all,
Like our love for the one who was born,
So we could celebrate the day of His birth,
Two thousand years ago on a glorious morn.

A SON NOT HIS OWN

He was deeply in love with his wife.
Their union would begin a happy home.
He has promised to love and support her,
But the child she carried was not his own.

She was a highly favored young woman.
The Holy Spirit the only touch she had known.
The vision of her life had now been changed,
As the child she carried was not his own.

She had prayed to her God for His guidance.
The angel came to Joseph when he was alone,
So he would know how it would come to be.
The child she carried would not be his own.

He felt it a privilege to be a good father.
The child grew up with others in the home.
He would train him in the ways of a carpenter.
No matter the child was never to be his own.

All things came together to change our world.
This child gave His life for our sins to atone.
I am sure the rewards are many for this father,
Who with God's help raised a son not his own.

HEARTS AND LOVE

Here it comes again, that celebration,
With those red hearts scattered all about.
You have to find a card and flowers,
Maybe some candy or jewelry to top it out.

These are good but do not prove love.
That should be done another way.
Like hold them when their heart hurts,
So you can help make it a better day.

Sometimes there is nothing to be said,
And there is nothing you can do.
Just be willing to always be there,
Patient, knowing they can turn to you.

Let each other know how much you care.
Just say "I love you" for no reason or rhyme.
Thank the Lord you have each other.
The Lord will make the place and time.

THINGS TO DO

I'm looking forward to our Christmas,
With our friends and family close around.
With all the plans that we have made,
In our hearts joy will be found.

There will be the things we always do,
In order to celebrate this special day.
Like food to cook and gifts to wrap,
And best wishes to send those far away.

Let us celebrate the birth of Jesus.
Our Lord born in the image of man.
He came to save us by endless grace,
And to hold us safe in His loving hand.

Think of those who do not have as much,
As the gracious Father has given you.

JUST TO REMEMBER

Long ago they began a journey,
In order to have the right to worship.
But many never reached our shores.
Sadly they would not survive the trip.

Some of us can trace our family's blood,
To the first ones to make it to this land.
Even those who came in recent years,
To face hardships we do not understand.

Many of us do not appreciate our freedom,
Or the heartbreak others gladly endured.
Because it was not our generation or time,
But with God their triumph was assured.

We must remember the trials they survived,
For the right to enjoy the life we now live.
To be able to realize the fruits of labor,
That faith in God and hard work will give.

In our hearts there will be many things,
That we can find to be thankful for.
Let that be the reason for this holiday,
And then you will enjoy it even more.

IT HAS BEEN TOLD

What can I tell you about this holiday
That someone has not told you before?
After all it's been two thousand years.
I don't know where to start anymore.

It is told He was born in a humble place,
Because there was no room at the inn.
The Son of God in the image of man.
The sweetest story that has ever been.

It is told that there were shepherds,
Tending sheep on hills outside of town.
Of angels who told them of our Jesus.
Who came to where the Baby was found.

It is told that Joseph protected his family,
And moved them quickly from danger.
It would be years before the wise men found,
The Precious Child that was born in a manger.

It is told that He gave His life for us,
To save our souls from eternal loss.
Of the blood and tears He would shed,
When He died for our sins on a cruel cross.

So let your thoughts be of His love for you,
  As you celebrate this wonderful time.
  We must forever keep this story alive.
It is a rewarding task, be it yours and mine.

THE COMING YEAR

"NEW YEARS DAY"

There are so many things that have happened,
To each of us throughout this year.
There was good and there has been the bad,
And through it all, He was always near.

We have all accomplished a lot this year.
Happy that we have grown closer to the Lord.
The love of friends and family holds us safe.
In our hearts, this can be just another reward.

We each have so much to look forward to,
As we welcome in another new year.
Things we should do to help each other,
As we trust in Him to make our pathway clear.

Resolutions made by man that are of his own needs,
Must be with the guidance found in God's grace.
Then we can expect His very best for each of us,
And know that everything will find its place.

Most of all is His intent that we find true peace.
Everything that happens will be for a reason.
We must simply trust in Him to safely lead us,
To find happiness and comfort in this season.

AFTER THE COLD

Today I walked outside in the sunshine.
It was warm and pleasant after the cold.
It's like maybe the world has been renewed.
To remind me of good things I have been told.

I know He will take care of me every day,
And there is always light at the end of night.
No matter how bad things may have been.
He is still in my heart and will make it right.

That I have great things yet to accomplish.
That He will be there to lead the way.
Though the pathway may not yet be clear,
Things will get better with each passing day.

I must get ready for a Christmas celebration.
I will be blessed to spend it with those I love.
They will be watching how I handle things.
The chance to show that my help is from above.

I will look forward to a new year to come.
He will give me things to do and words to say.
I pray that He will always hold me close,
With His help, no doubt I will find my way.

MY JESUS LIVES

EASTER

So much has been said about this special day.
A King with a crown of thorns to wear.
He died on a cross to redeem us from sin.
My Jesus with so much love to share.

There has never been one who cared so much.
Who already knew what His fate would be.
I know surely that if I had been the only sinner,
He still would have been willing to die for me.

There is no way I can ever hope to repay Him,
And I know He will never require that of me.
But He does merit my love and obedience,
To show by my life how others may be free.

We only need to trust by faith until He returns.
Then we will be able to see His loving hand.
It was scarred by a nail when He died for us,
So we would have a home in a peaceful land.

You see He returned to heaven to prepare it,
And He will provide for you this resting place.
Where you will never again know this world's trials,
And it can only be yours because of His grace.

WORDS TO THANK

"NINE ELEVEN"

This year they did not come easy like before.
I had to struggle for the right words to find.
It may be I do not understand His message.
The thoughts did not come easy to my mind.

Thanksgiving will be different than those before.
The world as we know it won't be the same.
But in my heart there is much to thank Him for.
And in quiet times I will still praise His name.

I did not lose one in the month of September.
But my eyes still sting and my heart still aches.
There are so many who must start over alone.
To find the awesome strength that survival takes.

I will not send one off to fight America's war.
But that does not remove it from my mind.
My lot will be to pray for their safe return.
Sons and daughters who fight for peace to find.

But no one has to go through this season alone.
He still loves us, and He will always be near.
The peace and joy we find will come from Him.
Thank Him for your blessings again this year.

A CHRISTMAS TO REMEMBER

Soon I'll go out and find the paper,
That I'll need to send this message to you.
For days thoughts have been on my mind.
But with me, this sort of thing is nothing new.

But my heart is not as happy as years before,
And now I often find myself in quiet reflection.
I am praying for those who must find strength,
So they can take their lives in a new direction.

I'll just have to go somewhere to a quiet place,
And patiently wait for the things I need to say.
It may be to just recall the story that's told,
Of how our Savior was born on Christmas day.

Just over two thousand years ago He came
Born in a manger, to Mary, God's Holy Son.
With Joseph who would raise Him as his own.
Jesus sent to redeem us, the Prophesied One.

So celebrate the birth of our Savior knowing
That He will shelter your path with His love.
That all the good that has happened to you,
Is because Jesus still watches from above.

PEACE IN THE YEAR

Ready or not here comes a new year.
Some are not through with this one yet.
Why do they feel there is so much undone?
They search for a peace they just can't get.

Could it be they are just not over the hurt?
Or still waiting for the other shoe to fall?
Why do they let worry control their life?
Why can't they just let Jesus handle it all?

I must admit I have found myself there too.
A feeling of not knowing, what else I can do.
I can't erase it from my mind that quickly.
I remember the horror of it all, just like you.

Most of us do not even know the heartache,
Of a season without the ones we hold dear.
Family gathered around us with a gentle touch.
We are getting ready for this brand-new year.

With God's help we have no other option.
We must learn to live our life in His care.
We must remember there has never been,
A time when He was not standing right there.

SIGNS OF THE TIMES

Holiday signs are early this year.
I can tell by the things I've started to see.
My cactus is ready to bloom again.
This plant constantly amazes me.

Do as I might, it does not get the message.
It's supposed to bloom a month from now.
I do what the book says about the time.
It's gonna bloom in November anyhow.

And then there's a beautiful poinsettia,
That's already topping out bright reds.
It is one I've had for years and years.
Pretty full leaves supporting its heads.

The nights are cool and days are clear.
An indication of what's going to be.
A day of giving thanks to our Father.
For the blessings He's given you and me.

Then on to the beautiful days of Christmas.
The joy of your family and friends nearby.
And we will celebrate God's love for man,
By the birth of His son, a gift for you and I.

CHRISTMAS GIFT

Although this is my yearly thing to do,
It was really easy to find the words to say.
Everything was here I needed to write this,
They just had to be placed a certain way.

Wishes are sent that come from the heart,
To let you know I am thinking of you.
I am hoping this has been a good year.
And rich blessings found their way through.

All the bad things that have happened,
If we let them will diminish the good.
That you can know when you have faith,
And a love for each other is understood.

You must never forget He cares for you.
He has kept you safe through the storm.
He has given you peace and comfort.
In His arms you can feel safe and warm.

The duty you have is simple and sweet.
Just tell the story of His miraculous birth.
Of how He came in the image of man,
And offers salvation to every person on earth.

JOY

As I start to write this letter, I remember,
This is a special time for me each year.
When I send a special greeting to say hello,
To friends and family that are far and near.

The signs of Christmas are with us again.
A time to celebrate our Master's birth.
There is a special feeling in our hearts.
On this day it is shown all over the earth.

It can be in the everyday things we do.
Just in the certain way we work and talk.
Even as we come together to worship Him,
And spread His joy in our daily walk.

The gathering of friends and our family.
Some we may not have seen for years.
The hugs and loving pats on the back.
The looks in their eyes and joyous tears.

The quiet times for our personal reflection,
Of just what this day was meant to be.
A day to remember why He came to earth.
To offer salvation to everyone, even me.

IT FEELS LIKE CHRISTMAS

Today it feels like Christmas will soon be here.
Beautiful songs are playing on the radio.
Tomorrow we will start to decorate the house.
Shopping needs to be done, next week I will go.

The weather has turned a little bit cooler.
Above me it is blue without a cloud in the sky.
It reminds me how it used to be in Virginia.
We will hear from Virginia friends by and by.

There will be the hurry and get it done in time,
Will it ever come together? I can only hope so.
But somehow it always seems to fall in place.
Take one day at a time is the only way I know.

Friends and family will grow even closer.
Possibly more than we have ever been before.
There have been times we needed each other.
Somehow we always manage to even the score.

Be sure and not let your heart fill with strife.
This is a season to spread joy and love to all
Just remember the reason for this holiday.
A tiny child born to a virgin in a cattle stall.

Jean Carley

IN THE MIDDLE

Here we are in the middle of the days,
That we used to celebrate this season.
We have had gatherings and prayers.
Knowing we must not forget the reason.

We enjoyed hearing from distant friends,
Even though it may even bring a tear.
But the joy of good memories abounds.
We have had of each other for another year.

Friends came to call, and we visited some.
Gifts were bountiful under our tree.
And things just fell into the right place.
There were so many blessings for me.

The tree still shines and the lights are on.
The cactus and poinsettia outdid themselves.
Our home is a place for the holiday spirit.
Decorations on all the tables and shelves.

We shared good moments with each other.
We kept secrets and hid things all around.
Now all the boxes have been taken away.
Wonder why my flip-flops can't be found.

THIS YEAR

Here we are in another brand-new year.
Seems as I get older they just fly by.
And things happen we do not understand.
I guess we're not supposed to know why.

Personally for us it's been a good year.
There have been some trials to overcome.
But we have never been left alone here.
God blessed us in more ways than some.

We pray God will shelter those we love.
Keep them from the harm that's out there.
Let them know that love is unconditional.
Their place in our hearts tells that we care.

Find the time to pray and wait on Him,
So His comfort and guidance we will see
Tell those around us what He can do,
And try our best to be where we need to be.

Give us tasks to do that make a difference.
Let us not look for praise or riches to find
Just live our lives the best we can every day.
Knowing if we honor Him, He will be kind.

GIFTS OF THE CHRISTMAS CHILD

We have received many gifts this year.
God has walked by our side every day.
Many wonderful things have happened.
To thank Him enough, there is no way.

Our children are healthy and happy.
Our family was blessed with a new one.
We can share a joy that lasts a lifetime,
With the special love of daughters and a son.

We walked in a valley for a time this year.
There was a great trial we overcame.
We knew prayers would make a difference.
Loved ones joined us to call on His name.

We were able to help others in their pain,
We prayed and kept them in our heart.
With God's help we made a difference.
He made a pathway for us to do our part.

As everyday life continues here on earth,
Be reminded of all that needs to be done.
In your heart you must be ever thankful,
When God allows you to be that special one.

This is because of the Christmas Child,
Whose birth we shall honor this day.
Never has a Gift been more special,
One that can never be taken away.

NEXT YEAR TO COME

It's late in the day on this New Year's Eve.
Many thoughts and memories come to mind.
You see it's been a year for the record books.
There was good and the bad that we can find.

But through it all God walked by our side.
We were never alone through the valley deep.
Friends and family prayed and waited nearby.
And when it was over our victory was sweet.

We must be thankful He found us worthy
Many lessons were learned this past year.
No matter how bad you think things are,
You can rely on God, and he will be near.

Again our soldiers fight a war on foreign soil.
We lose young men and women every day.
We must pray that this world can find peace.
That our God will show our leaders the way.

I lost the dearest friend I had in Virginia.
He went to be with Jesus on Christmas Eve.
His family will gather and hold each other.
Nothing should stop this, they have to grieve.

I thank my God every day for what I have.
Good that happens is of His unending grace.
So help your neighbor to travel in his valley,
But for the grace of God you could be in his place.

EVERY CHRISTMAS

All of a sudden you find it is upon you.
You do not think you will get it done.
There is so much to be taken care of.
All the things to do and you are the one.

But this has been a year of good jobs done,
And helping each other for the good of all.
Of closer relationships with good friends,
And helping neighbors when they call.

This is what we do with joy in our hearts.
That is the way it is supposed to be.
We do not work for man's hollow praise.
The Father's payment is sufficient for me.

I would wish for each of you joy and peace.
That your family will hold you close in love.
And you and yours find contentment today,
And rest from our Heavenly Father above.

These are the things that happen every year.
In their own way they help define the season.
It is your own responsibility to never forget
The birth of a Child is really the reason

THIS YEAR TO ANOTHER

It is peaceful here this last day of the year.
Things around me are quiet and serene.
It is as if the world is at peace with nature.
Out my back door I find a beautiful scene.

It is hidden from the world's strife and chaos.
I thank my Heavenly Father for His care.
He has protected my loved ones from harm.
And we look forward to a brand-new year.

But my heart remembers all those who suffer.
I wonder why so many have to be lost.
I can only imagine their heartache and pain.
And why so many must pay such a cost.

But it is not my time to understand why.
I can only pray for those in peril today.
And know it is God's divine intervention,
Which will ultimately show them His way?

I would wish peace that comes from the Father
Contentment that only His grace can afford.
Love of your fellow man to give you happiness.
And joy when you are in the care of the Lord.

AFTER THE FIRST DAY

Today while on our usual morning walk,
We met a friend we often see along the way.
He said good morning and Happy New Year.
His friendly greeting helped to make our day.

It dawned on me how we choose to celebrate.
This is a holiday that was created by man.
One that simply honors a day in the year.
Not a special birth or death as we often can.

If we just extended the feeling of Christmas.
Celebrate the joy of giving from the heart.
The days before Christmas are so commercial.
It would give the new year a sweeter start.

What I am trying to say in this message.
Remember what His life was all about.
Giving, joy, compassion, peace, and love.
Things a happy life does not exist without.

Maybe keep the Christmas spirit a little longer.
Just be a little nicer down life's road somehow.
Thank God for His gift that saved your soul,
And the feeling that is in your heart just now.

THE HOLIDAY CONES

With all the rain we've had around this place,
I'm lucky to be able to find our backyard.
But I was out there looking at growing things.
My thought, no water, shouldn't be that hard.

I have this pine tree in a garden out there.
It is a stray that was never meant to be.
You see my husband wants no trees in the yard.
But then one day it was there, growing free.

I guarded that tree and put a wall around it.
I planted flowers to bloom and keep it company.
Not much can grow out there in our backyard,
But just maybe God put it there for me to see.

Over the years it has reached up straight and tall.
He commented when things started growing there.
It weathered storms, heat, and sometimes drought,
And now he helps me when I need to take care.

Today I went to look for pinecones for the table.
The fresh ones just always look better each year.
Now we will soon celebrate the Lord's birthday.
I found them, beautiful ones, they were right there.

THANK YOU FATHER

We have much to be thankful for this season.
There were storms, but they did not come here.
We need to pray for those less fortunate.
For many souls it has been a terrible year.

We have much to look forward to this year.
There will be gatherings with friends we love.
We will hold them close and share the warmth,
And feel the blessings from our Father above.

Families will again be together for this holiday.
They don't see each other the rest of the year.
It is the only time they are in the same place.
They make the most of it, maybe shed a tear.

There will be new children you have not met.
How others will have grown, you will not believe.
And some you may have lost along the way.
In your heart you will find the time to grieve.

This day was created by man to thank our Father.
For all He does for us each and every day.
Let your thanksgiving be genuine from the heart.
A special time for America to be still and pray.

CACTUS SEASON

It happens every year that plant just goes crazy.
It's supposed to bloom for the holiday to come.
Not show off on my back porch right now.
Among all the plants I grow, this one is dumb.

But it is beautiful you see, just full of buds.
And I will watch it rule the porch in all its glory.
Tomorrow one or two buds will burst into color,
And it will be the center of another yuletide story.

Some things just come early to get us ready,
For the reason we celebrate this time of year.
It is a time we should be remembering the joys,
And join in thanks with all those we hold dear.

Before long our decorations will be put out,
And neighbor's houses will be covered with lights
Cookies will be baked and cards will be mailed.
We'll make trips around town to enjoy the sights.

All these things we do every year at this time.
As we celebrate the birth of our Precious Lord.
Just make sure your hearts know the reason,
So we can worship Him together in one accord.

THE FACE OF CHRISTMAS

The spirit of Christmas arrived early this year,
And I am looking forward to the things we do.
Like getting out all the decorations and lights,
And writing my yearly Christmas card to you.

I've already been shopping a time or two,
And so far the experience has been a good one.
People are friendly but some still amaze me.
Like every year I will be glad when it is done.

This year there has been sadness in my heart.
I have friends who still struggle with grief.
But I will patiently stand with them in prayer,
And I know that Jesus will send His relief.

Just know that in my heart I am thinking of you,
And as I sign this card I can see your face.
And one of the things that gives my heart joy,
Is that God put me here in this time and place.

I would wish for you the peace of Christmas,
That comes when you remember Jesus birth.
It is His walk to the cross that sealed our future,
And His bountiful love for everyone on earth.

PART OF THE CELEBRATION

How on earth did it get here so quick?
Everything is gone from under the tree.
All of a sudden Christmas has gone.
My home is quiet, how can this be?

Today we celebrated His birthday.
I thought of it as the day progressed.
And just how great His bounty was,
And just how much we have been blessed.

And I had my children close around me.
We had good times and love to share.
We talked of times that we remember,
Bound by the knowledge we really care.

Things will start to get back to normal.
We will get ready to welcome a new year.
We have made promises that we will keep.
We will be closer to those we hold dear.

For each of you I wish a Happy New Year
If you made a promise, then see it through.
Make an effort to be there for loved ones.
Those in your life who mean the most to you.

WISH ME MERRY CHRISTMAS

This year please wish me Merry Christmas.
No season's greetings or happy holidays.
I just want to remember what this day is for.
Do not chide if I want to celebrate this way.

The story of Christ's birth will never change,
And I respect the traditions of other I meet.
But why should I change my worship of Him,
While in my daily life other people I will greet?

My message to you will be from my heart,
And I will hope you have a wonderful day.
And all the family traditions you celebrate,
Will be remembered in a special way.

But imagine how wonderful it would be to hear,
Merry Christmas from strangers you see.
With a smile on their face that really glows,
And a voice of love, that's how it should be.

So this is it, I renewing my commitment,
And as I send this letter I can see your face.
Together we celebrate the birth of our Savior,
And remember His gift, His abundant grace.

THIS YEAR TO COME

Some times in your life are better than others.
Mostly you just take life from day to day.
There are times when your heart will break.
But by trusting in the Lord you find your way.

This year things happened that tore at my heart.
But Christmas was good, our loved ones are well.
We are looking forward to the year to come.
Whatever God has in store in time He will tell.

God has allowed me to help in times of need,
And to be ready when I needed to go to them.
He has taught me that I will never stand alone
And allowed me to sit quietly and wait on Him.

If you are my friend, I hope I helped in some way.
If only a fleeting tiny word or some meager deed
To have lifted your spirits or lightened your day
Or that you know I will be there whatever the need.

I wish for everyone true contentment in their life.
That God will take their burdens and set them free.
That they will be given the chance to help others,
That where they are is where they want to be.

SEVEN/FOUR/SEVEN

This Fourth of July will not be so different,
Than the ones we celebrate each year.
We must continue to pray for our nation,
Even while we may quietly shed a tear.

As a nation we have known a storm or two.
We may find an unwanted ache in our heart.
But we must support and pray for our leaders,
Then we pick up, dust off, and get a new start.

You must remember why we have this holiday.
And try to do what we can to make it right.
Pray earnestly for God's leadership and grace.
Show support of country with all your might.

Do not take the efforts of brave men for granted.
Without them our freedom would be lost.
We must be willing to guard it every day
By remembering those who paid the cost.

We must show our enemies we stand firm.
And try to return to what we used to be.
A nation founded on Christian faith and honor.
So we can always be the land of the free.

DUTY OF THE FOURTH

I am proud of the flag that shadows my yard.
It flies high and bright for the world to see.
It is the symbol of my country's birthday,
That over two hundred years ago came to be.

This country was formed by men of God,
Who believed in the commitment they signed.
They invited Him to lead them to the future,
So a better life in America they would find.

Our Constitution must forever stand.
That is what we will celebrate on this day.
Never forget the price that had to be paid,
By the lives that had to fall along the way.

Today soldiers fight for freedoms we enjoy,
And they do it in a distant foreign land.
Defending the rights we take for granted,
So we will not see the enemy close at hand.

We must keep the story of this country alive.
Do not let the praises grow dim in our memory.
It is a task that is up to every one of us,
To be an example for the whole world to see.

MEMORIES

This will not be just another Memorial Day.
Of late memories have brought to my mind,
Things of past years I find are important.
I need not search; they are easy to find.

Recent days brought some bittersweet tears,
But times with family and friends were good.
We drew comfort from each other every day,
And the down times we certainly understood.

I have created another book of memories,
That will give me comfort that I can share.
Of one who gave his life for his fellow man,
Who in the shadow of wrong chose to care.

We are fighting in a foreign troubled land.
A war that many think is not for good cause.
Just think of all of those who bravely go,
To answer the nation's call without a pause.

Remember ones who will never come home.
Who will leave wives and children alone.
Of mothers and fathers, sisters and brothers.
The bravery of a soldier forever to be known.

THE FLAG OF THE FOURTH

This Fourth will be better than before,
Even with all the sadness we will find here.
We still have things to be thankful for.
We can honor our flag openly without fear.

Please hold up the flag of this country.
Give it the honor you know it is due.
The reason for colors from which it is made,
And for the patriots who died for you.

The right to worship God as we choose;
We are numbered among a precious few.
A quiet time of prayer for our country,
Will be the very least that you can do.

No matter what you think about my America,
I am proud to live in the land of the free.
There can be no better place on this earth,
Another blessing that my God gives me.

We need faith in a God that sustains us,
And gives hope when others let us down.
No matter how deep our sorrows may go,
Direction from God can still be found.

GEORGIA THANKSGIVING

Maybe we have to look a little harder,
Than we have in years gone by.
To find things to be thankful for,
But every day we must surely try.

Some families will not have shelter,
Or food for their children to eat.
With bills they would like to pay,
But with no funds, they cannot meet.

Find a way to make a life better,
Like be there for your fellow man.
And do something for someone else,
In a special way that only you can.

Be amazed at how good you will feel,
When you go for the extra mile.
To lift one up who needs your help,
So they can have a reason to smile.

Thank God for everything you have.
It is by His grace that you are here.
With all the things that are wrong today,
He's blessed you; it's been a good year.

IT WAS TOLD

It was always known that it would happen.
That Jesus would come down to the earth.
It was always known how it would happen.
That He would come through a virgin birth.

We learned from early Bible teachings,
As it was told hundreds of years before.
That a messiah would come to die for us.
Sin would not have dominion any more.

He knew how his life on earth would end.
That he would be nailed on a cross to die.
No matter how much He tried to tell them,
Some still would never understand why.

Let us always remember how He loves us,
And what He was willing to do for man.
A wonderful gift we could never imagine,
Salvation, paid for by nails in His hands.

Celebrate His birth with your loved ones.
Make it a time to spread joy and love.
If His presence lives in your heart,.
Your gift will be a blessing from above.

TOGETHER

There are lots of things about this day,
That your love should bring to mind.
A time for each and every one of you,
To remember good things you can find.

Love for each other is blessed by God.
He is happy when he is head of your home.
When you allow Him to guide your way,
Peace and contentment will be known.

No two relationships will be the same.
You must make your own path to walk.
Just remember you are to be as one.
Never miss a chance to just stop and talk.

Thing how long you have been together.
Just when and how it started years ago.
When you asked the Heavenly Father
To show the way that you should go.

It's all right for hearts and flowers,
To have a special place in your love.
Just as long as you never forget,
Your union is blessed by God above.

THANKSGIVING'S HISTORY

There are a lot of things to be thankful for.
Tell of history that brought us to this place.
And for the pilgrims who came before us,
Supported by God's leadership and grace.

At that time life revolved around survival.
The harsh winter claimed more than a few.
They ventured to a new world sight unseen.
But it was what they knew they had to do.

We do not know how life would be today,
If they had not had the courage to prevail.
Only the Heavenly Father knew for sure,
And He was with them when they set sail.

Do not grow weary of thanking God.
You have been blessed to live in the USA.
And remember how He still cares for us,
Now as we are struggling to find our way.

Never forget those who protect our freedom,
With dedication and loyalty in their heart.
They fight in foreign trenches every day.
The honor they are due, where do you start?

Pray for our country now more than ever.
And that our leaders will earnestly try,
To make the decisions that they should,
So she will be a beacon as in days gone by.

CHRISTMAS—A STORY

First I want to wish you a Merry Christmas.
I hope all has been well with you this year.
We have spent time with family and friends.
We laughed with some and others shed a tear.

Some of our family was lost along the way;
But others have joined to make it grow.
Now new traditions will sweeten our lives.
And our hearts will have new joys to know.

Houses are alive with holly and candles;
Happy children with lights in their eyes.
Parents and kids keeping secrets until,
The day which brings a sweet surprise.

I have visions of a mother and baby;
Of shepherds on a hill watching sheep;
Of wise men who came to see this child,
And a wonderful secret they had to keep.

He would live just more than thirty years,
And He would die to save my soul.
And for that I must be eternally grateful;
For His entire lifetime, that was His goal.

SUNDAY SUNRISE

I must send you something for Easter,
Just to let you know I am thinking of you.
Maybe I don't stay in touch like I should,
And this is the best thing I can do.

We tend to get too busy as days go by,
With no time for things we should do.
It is on our hearts, but we don't do it,
Yet in my mind I have a vision of you.

I know how you will celebrate Easter.
I know where you will be at daybreak.
And I know how you will worship Him.
Blessings will be there for you to take.

I know you will remember the reason,
That we celebrate this reverent event.
We will bow our heads in prayer and thanks.
For His only Son, our Heavenly Father sent.

This story has been the same for centuries.
No one else could atone for our sin.
Just remember in your heart on this day,
We are forgiven, no matter where we've been.

THE FOURTH OF
TWENTY TEN

I know in my heart I need to write,
Something about our state of affairs.
So many are discouraged and worried,
And think government no longer cares.

We have come to think that there is no hope.
If we sit by the wayside it just may be true.
But changes can still turn things around,
And these changes could depend on you.

Americans are not willing to be defeated,
Without standing side by side to fight.
Just be reminded of what we believe in.
It hasn't changed, just don't lose sight.

We still have the right to mark a ballot,
And it may take some time to get it done.
But if we don't start right now to do it,
We cannot put the blame on anyone.

We must again seek leadership from God,
Just as our fathers did so many years ago.
Then stand on God's eternal promise to answer,
So that in the end His victory we will know.

PEACE ON THANKSGIVING DAY

Today the sun shines bright out front.
A blue cloudless sky over the rooftop.
It is a quiet and peaceful world.
It is as if everything decided to stop.

A gentle breeze is softly scattering leaves.
My maple tree will soon be all but bare.
The nights are cool but days are warm.
Life seems to be moving without a care.

Our children told us they are coming.
It will be wonderful to just have them here.
It's been too long since we embraced.
Things will be remembered for another year.

Soon we will celebrate Thanksgiving again.
Because our forefathers believed in Him.
They came here to worship as they believed.
And with His care He watched over them.

Thank God every day for our America.
It was His divine will that we be here.
With all the things that are wrong today,
He's blessed you; it's been a good year.

CHRISTMAS THIS YEAR

What can I say about Christmas this year
That will be different than those before?
The story as we know it has not changed.
We all have memories our hearts can store.

This year we could try to make a difference.
Just maybe someone who needs a new start.
If it takes some time and a bit of effort,
Contentment will find a place in your heart.

Maybe you could start with your family.
One you have not seen or talked to for a while.
One who needs something only you can provide,
Or a tender touch to show your love for a child.

Usually a gift from the heart will do wonders.
Something that's special that only you can do.
This wonderful gift will then change your life,
And make a special memory just for you.

When you tell the Christmas story just remember,
That Christ did all of these things while on earth.
And never forget when you say Merry Christmas,
The gift of salvation was the reason for His birth.

About the day that's about to be.
How He gets me up and gets me going,
And thankful He still takes care of me.

RESURRECTION

Today we will celebrate in memory,
What my Jesus did for you and me.
How he was tortured, bled and died,
So we would forever be set free.

We can only envision in our minds,
The terrible price He had to pay.
It was His choice to do this for you,
So you can celebrate a resurrection day.

Because of His unmerited love for you,
There is nothing that you can do.
That will ever balance the justice scale,
But that will never be required of you.

This is a story of two thousand years,
That will never change come what may.
It is embedded in our hearts and souls,
And comes to our memory every day.

Do not grow weary of telling this story,
Or let it be a song that you may sing.
So they will know everlasting salvation,
And peace that only His love can bring.

A DAY TO HONOR

This time of year I always want to write,
About something that stays on my mind.
How many lost their lives over the years,
And I look in my heart for words to find.

I'll begin with memories we all share.
Over years the people we have known.
The families of loved ones that we lost.
Love and compassion that was shown.

We gather where the valiant come,
And give them the honor they deserve.
A flag is folded and taps ring out;
The final tribute to those who serve.

I have felt the searing pain of loss,
For one of those who chose not to stay.
And knew the road that he should take,
But he is not where his body will lay.

You see, I know their lives are with the Lord,
And they are forever in a peaceful place.
I feel it is a beautiful garden of honor.
It's just for them because of God's grace.

STORIES TO TELL

Now is a time we can be thankful,
For all the good that's come our way.
Someone is now home safe and sound.
It will be a wonderful Christmas day.

Soon distant children will come home.
It is a visit we've waited for all year.
We will pray for safe traveling mercies.
There will be so many stories to hear.

Our home will become a celebration,
Of the joyous Christmas season.
We will light a tree and show His love,
And never forget the wonderful reason.

We will gather at our church in prayer,
As we remember those in need.
We will try to make their load lighter,
If their spiritual hunger we can feed.

We will see the antics of happy children,
And the innocence found on their faces.
All the wonder the season affords them,
The heart of a child sees it in many places.

So please wish me a Merry Christmas.
It will put a good feeling in my heart.
I will promise to do the same for you,
Then a true Christmas season will start.

Please join with us in a simple prayer,
That our friends and family will see.
The joy and peace that Jesus gives,
A Christmas blessing for you and me.

TO BE THANKFUL

There are things we must always remember.
Reasons why we celebrate this day each year.
For the very foundation of our United States
Was based on a desire to worship without fear.

This story has been told to us so many times,
It is burned in our memory as if we were there.
Hardships they overcame make ours grow pale.
They survived by their determination and prayer.

We are blessed in more ways than we can count.
We still worship in the manner of our choice.
We have told the entire world how it should be.
When a government listens to a voter's voice.

Again our soldiers fight wars on foreign soil.
We lose young men and women every day.
Their families know a grief to their very soul.
From deep in your heart find the words to pray.

We have so much to be thankful for this year.
God has been there for each and every one.
True, there have been mountains for us to climb.
But with God's help we saw the battles won.

SPECIAL PEOPLE

COMING HOME

MISSIONARIES

For hours on end I tried to write,
A message about your coming home.
And I knew the words would come to me,
If I just spent some quiet time alone.

We will be so glad to have you here,
Close by where we can see and touch.
To share all the good news we have,
Because we have missed so much.

You are such a special part of our life.
In spirit we have always been close by.
Our prayers have always been with you.
In your heart you know the reason why.

We do not want to interfere with plans.
You will have so many things to do.
But just remember when you have time,
We would love to just sit and be with you.

So somewhere in the not too distant future,
When things have finally settled down.
We will talk and laugh and maybe even cry.
It will be so great just to have you around.

Maybe even when you just need to rest,
And you need to find a place to get away.
Come here, it will be as if you are home.
This will be the place for a peaceful day.

THE LEAVING

MISSIONARIES

We knew you would leave again,
And go back to where you feel you must.
We do not have to be happy about it.
That will not be required of us.

We know what you do is your calling.
We each have our own things to do;
Each in our very own special way.
This work has been assigned to you.

It is our task to always pray for you,
And support you the best we can.
Only together can we get it done.
Telling of God's grace and love for man.

So go to where you need to be,
And do the task you have been told.
While we stay here and wait for you,
With only memories left to hold.

We must say we have been happy,
Spending this time with you.
It was so great to have you here,
Now go with God, your work to do.

THE PRIVILEGE OF CAMELOT

THE KENNEDY'S

They were all born into a life of privilege.
It comes to our mind's eye as we recall.
The way they lived their lives to the fullest,
And have care for each other through it all.

In their world life was different from most.
They appeared to answer to no one.
They would always depend on each other,
And when it was needed, they got it done.

You hardly ever saw them shed a tear.
They retreated to private places to mourn.
This was the life they had chosen to live,
Sometimes subjected to ridicule and scorn.

They are again deep in the valley of grief.
What has happened they could not control.
Another time there is no avenue of escape.
Another cutting tragedy will take its toll.

I have watched them over the last few days,
As they privately went to God in prayer.
He will comfort hearts, He will ease the pain.
He will strengthen their souls with loving care.

At some time Camelot may have to end,
And we may never know when or why.
But there is sadness in a corner of my heart.
And I know that but for the grace of God go I.

A JOY FOR LIVING

You are a constant inspiration to me.
You always have a smile to give.
Things you do, the love you show,
Is reflected in the life you live.

You are surely a constant light to me.
I stand and watch the things you do.
Always helping the ones around you,
On darkest days you pull them through.

You carry burdens with a joyful heart.
Life's problems do not get you down.
I never know when your heart hurts,
Because of the joy you spread around.

I do not know what we would do,
If your pleasant smile I could not see.
Or the ways you always make me think,
Things are not as bad as they could be.

You do not judge your fellow man.
You find good in everyone you know.
You are never too busy to stop and talk.
Concern for others you always show.

Do not ever change a single thing.
I will delight in your gracious smile.
I will always love you as you are,
Always willing to go the extra mile.

You are my friend
Just how blessed can I be?
There is no answer.

A PLACE TO GO

MISSIONARY LIFE

We are going to miss you when you leave.
You were given a job, and you did it well.
We have been blessed by your being here.
What is to happen now, time will tell.

We are not to question what is to be.
It was always part of the Master's plan.
It shall be our task to continue the work.
By faith in God, we are assured we can.

Because of your leadership and care.
We are equipped to handle the task.
Do not ever take us from your prayers.
We will remember you, you need not ask.

All the accolades will be welcome.
Most of them you will always recall.
What you have given was from your heart.
And it is that which means the most of all.

So go where it is you feel you have to be.
After all man cannot tell you what to do.
And man cannot tell you where to go.
We must understand God is calling you.

LAURA'S PRAYER

THE OLYMPICS

They said she had no chance to win.
She was just too far down the line.
There were so many ahead of her.
Quite possibly this was not her time.

All she wanted was to do her dives.
Her smile told the world I know I can.
She was a picture of quiet talent.
She was not swayed by words of man.

I say my prayers to give me power.
I think of all that I'm told to do.
I give it my all from deep in my soul,
And knowing to myself I will be true.

God was there to put my fears to rest,
And he gave me peace of mind.
Only by His grace did I win the gold.
If I trust in Him, He is always kind.

THE HEALER'S TOUCH

In everyone's path there are special people,
Who can do their job exceptionally well.
The encouragement that things will get better,
Knowing the final outcome may be hard to tell.

The advice and opinions that help the healing.
Praise for doing better than expected means more.
The patience and understanding when it is needed.
The replies to questions asked many times before.

These things are not taught but rather are found,
In the heart of the doctor when he cares for you.
When he knows how much hangs in the balance,
In the end how much depends on what you can do.

The doctor knows that God has ultimate control.
Over what the final outcome is going to be.
Unknown to most, he may have said a prayer,
Quietly asking for a healing that he can see.

Now I ask that you stand near and watch for him
That in the future as he finds the way he must go
The healer's touch means more because you care.
Whatever happens then, contentment he will know.

ROSE ON A LAMP

It came to me as a gift of appreciation.
A small thing with a rose on the front.
It needed work but that's fine with me.
A new cord and a lampshade to hunt.

Now it graces a place of honor,
In a room where my memories abide.
Of family history and remembered love.
It sets in a place to be shown with pride.

I was in the presence of angels.
As they came to take her home to rest.
I was able to let her go with them,
Knowing in the end she would be blest.

When I look at it, I will always remember,
A sweet smile and piercing blue eyes.
Of a time I was afforded the chance,
To make a difference in others' lives.

Come to my home to see this gift.
In honor of a woman who left her stamp,
On my heart so I would remember her.
Since she once owned a beautiful lamp.

YOUR PRESENCE

A CARING DOCTOR

In everyone's life there are exceptional people,
And you will meet them in your everyday walk.
Some may not have made such a great impression.
Some are only remembered by how they talk.

Some are remembered by their quiet presence.
You are awed when they come into view.
You may never have a chance to speak to them,
But years later their memory will be with you.

Most have a profession where good is done,
If they do it well they are mostly content.
Some go through life searching for prestige.
In the end so many wasted years are spent.

Remember you must stop and take time to think,
Of all the good you are allowed to do each day.
You have every reason to stand tall and proud.
People are changed by what you do and say.

Prayers of friends and family were answered.
Even though we walked in the valley for a bit.
Our Heavenly Father has completed a healing,
And you were one of those He used to do it.

DISTANT FRIENDS

You show up from time to time around here,
And you are always a joy for us to see.
Your friendly smiles and loving hugs,
Always make the day nicer for me.

Things tend to happen while we are apart,
At these times we wish we were nearer.
So we would be able to hold and comfort.
Then when we meet the time is dearer.

We see your faces with love in your eyes.
If there is concern, we know it is true.
We talk of how God takes care of us.
When we are apart we pray for you.

In a way we share children and family.
They are important to us in a special way.
We care for them and hold them close.
They have no choice; we are here to stay.

We must make a promise in our hearts,
Because our lives are so much the same.
Never will we let go of this special bond.
We are family in heart if not in name.

A MAN OF GOD—A LEGACY

In everyone's life there are exceptional people.
Put there because of God's unending grace.
They do not give you the option to fail.
In his world failure did not have a place.

No matter how bad life's blows were dealt,
He always saw a light at the end of the lane.
It was never his lot to stand to the side,
And leave someone alone to bear their pain.

There are times in life I will never forget,
Of all the good this man was allowed to do.
I can picture his face in my mind just now.
As he was used by God to pull me through.

The people he helped cannot be numbered.
Probably more than anyone will ever know.
A quiet example to everyone he ever met,
How the love of God in his face could show.

He has a very special place to be just now.
It is quiet and peaceful, and there we will meet.
His crowns in heaven cannot be numbered.
He is ready to lay them at His Master's feet.

It is your lot to draw strength from knowledge.
How he touched your life each and every day.
Remember how he would want you to live.
Just ask our Heavenly Father to show the way.

THE GIPPER'S JOURNEY

RONALD REAGAN

For the past few days I've watched the pageantry,
And the honor bestowed upon one of our own.
I am reminded how a nation can come together,
To support a matriarch who is now left alone.

I have seen the strength that only God can give,
To a woman who stood by her husband in love.
Who saw him through the sunset of his life,
And upheld her vows honored by God above.

I hope it brings us closer together as a country,
And makes us stop and think about what is good.
Two people under God's love created an atmosphere,
Where love and respect for each other was understood.

A man who quietly led the most powerful nation,
From a cold war into the bright freedom of rebirth.
Who by communication and wisdom overcame,
A division that had for decades shadowed the earth.

He was no more than many men could hope to be.
It was just that God chose to put him in that place.
And the good he did and the peace that he won,
He credited to the Heavenly Father's wonderful grace.

He will be a memory we will put away with others
Now that he has moved to a better world in peace.
We should go on as a nation that can be led by God.
To be an example of good that should never cease.

THE FOLDED CLOTH

MEMORIES OF A FORMER PASTOR

I see your hand with the folded cloth
Go to your face to wipe away the tears.
You always have it near for a purpose.
Something you have used over the years.

It is always near you next to your folder,
Or off to the left ready for your hand to reach.
You are not ashamed to show true emotion.
This is a like my own father would teach.

I often remember his tender, caring nature.
How he always had time to calm my fears.
In his pocket he always had a folded cloth,
That more than once wiped away my tears.

I know your heart cares for us as your flock,
And you love our Father above so much.
You remember the cost of your salvation,
And you often know of the Savior's touch.

I remember how you lay it on your Bible,
When you invite us to make a choice.
I think this memory will always be with me.
A part of you, like the sound of your voice.

GOD GOES TO A BALL GAME

LITTLE LEAGUE–WORLD CHAMPS

I have watched the games with pride,
As our boys slowly marched to the top.
They were the best in the world no doubt.
Deliberate and precise, they did not stop.

They did not accept that they might lose.
It was not a word they chose to hear.
But even if they had not reached their goal,
It would have been a wonderful year.

They showed compassion for the losers,
That probably only a true American would.
They were not ashamed to comfort them,
In the way that only a true winner could.

Parents cheered and beamed with pride,
As they watched their sons do their part.
To bring the banners home to Georgia,
With pride in each and every boy's heart.

Then yesterday God went to a ball game,
And He knew what would come to be.
That a youngster would say a prayer,
Then hit a home run for the world to see.

THE PREACHER

The preacher, he can sneak up on you,
Because he is a quiet gentle soul.
But he does not intend to intrude;
He just blends in, that is his goal.

He stands next to the ones he loves,
Often with an impish look on his face.
Waiting for a chance to make you smile,
Or just maybe put you in your place.

I do know he can do that if he chooses,
And you will never know it's done.
You stop to think what happened here?
Then you realize it was done in fun!

It is easy to make him laugh at things.
And he praises you for a job well done.
And in the end that is all you need,
That he thinks you are a special one.

He is one of God's working children,
And his job will never be done.
That is what a Baptist minister does.
This is true because I know he is one.

Just doing his job, a.k.a, Fearless Leader

WHO GOD BLESSES

In this life people are set before us,
With an endless amount of love to give.
To help us handle the hard times,
And an example of how we should live.

One who has an endless amount of faith,
That allows them to finish their task.
They know things that need to be done,
And they are completed before you ask.

You are impressed with their courage.
You are in awe of the depth of their love.
Most often their face is on your mind,
Because they are blessed from above.

There are not many people like them.
They should be honored as a true friend.
One you know you can always count on,
To be there for whatever life may send.

This is the description of a worker for Christ
Outstanding in the true sense of the word.
A person who lives in the shelter of Jesus,
Of whose good deeds you many never have heard.

OLD FRIENDS

It takes a long time to grow old friends.
You have to work on it all life long.
But it's one of the joys in your life.
It's like sweet words to an old song.

Though miles may come between you,
In your thoughts you are never far apart.
You are constantly on each other's mind.
There are sweet memories in your heart.

There are times known only to you,
That you have shared over many years.
You stood with each other in hard times.
You comforted when there were fears.

We quietly watched your family change,
As children grew up to be on their own.
We were granted a very special honor,
That few outsiders will have ever known.

There are things shared just between us,
That many may not even know about.
And that's okay; it's just ours to remember.
Sweet prayers, loving things, no doubt.

THE PATRIOT GUARD

They were there to protect him,
As he went home for his final ride.
They will offer honor and respect,
In peace and dignity they will abide.

They will protect them in their grief,
And allow them to send him on his way.
To a loving, gracious Heavenly Father,
In whose arms he will forever stay.

This young man died for his country.
A higher calling is hard for us to find.
There are those who would dishonor him.
Do not cross the Guard, they will not be kind.

It is from their hearts that they do this.
Many have served their country well.
They answered the call without a thought
And they came home with stories to tell.

After their appointed duty is completed,
They will return to life just like you and I.
Quietly they walk among us every day.
Proud Americans, don't even ask why.

Jean Carley

THE LIFETIME OF A VETERAN

The other day I stood on the roadside.
As a returning soldier passed by.
I prayed for comfort for his family.
I held a flag; there was a tear in my eye.

This day will be hard for those parents.
They still have vivid memories of their son.
There will be no way to ease their pain.
Only in their mind were his battles won.

Veterans live and walk among us every day.
Some of them are right here in this place.
We will never forget their faithful service.
They are here by God's perfect grace.

Many quietly go about their daily tasks.
They worship God and pay their dues.
They work hard to support their families.
They have a shoulder a youngster can use.

A smile or nod from you is all they need,
To let them know that you really do care.
And that the future of our great country,
Is a responsibility that each of us share.

WALKING WITH
THE LORD

MY LORD AND I

There are so many times each day
when I just stop and think,
Of how much I have and how much I am blessed.
How the Lord is taking care of me
and watching every move.
Keeping me safe from harm and sending joy my way.

There are so many times each day
when I just stop and think.
Of how He has looked over me
when troubles came my way,
Or when things go well for no reason other than,
I just knew He had to have been
there watching over me.

There are so many times each day
when I just stop and think.
Amazed at how well things go for
me and know He has a hand,
In the overall things which make up
my days and all my times.
When I look back I just have to
stop and thank Him, quietly.

There are so many times each day
when I just stop and think.
Of how much I need Him, how I could
not survive without His care.
I cannot picture my life without Him
and what He does for me.
The times I can use to help oth-
ers which give joy to my heart.

There are so many times each day
when I just stop and think.
That I must not take the credit for
the good I do for others.
Without Him in my heart directing my every thought.
I would not be the person I am with
much room yet to praise.

There are so many times each day
when I just stop and think.
Of all the wonderful things I can do
that will make a difference,
In someone's life as they are walking along with me.
He guides me you know. I can-
not take the credit; it is to His glory

THE SEARCH

I've never felt so homeless,
As I do right now.
Like I need to go somewhere,
But I'm just not sure where.

I've never felt so homeless,
As I do right now.
There are lots of doors that open,
But do I dare go there?

I've never felt so homeless,
As I do right now.
It's like I'm wasting my time,
And something needs to be done.

I never felt so homeless,
As I do right now.
Like I need to be at peace,
And I just don't want to wait.

I've never felt so homeless,
As I do right now.
I know I'm secure in Jesus.
But I'm just outside the door.

I've never felt so homeless,
As I do right now.
Jesus, take my hand, show me,
Where do I go from here?

Make me feel safe again.
Give me things to do,
With a family of God's children.
Then I will be home again.

PROTECTION

Lord, please repair the cracks in my armor.
Do not let Satan in.
He seeks to destroy my confidence,
And lead me back to sin.

Lord, please protect me from doubts and fears.
Do not let go of my hand.
Let it be you I am depending on,
And not the wiles of man.

Lord, please take care of those I love down here.
Stretch out your loving arm,
That will lead them into your fold,
So they'll be safe from harm.

Lord, let me find direction from your word,
So everything falls in place.
And I find comfort that I need,
Encircled by your grace.

Lord, let me be a light to others near my path,
Keep me quiet when I need to be.
Let me know how best to listen,
Then I will abide in peace with thee.

WAITING FOR HIS MESSAGE

I will sit quietly; the Lord will tell me what to say.
Somehow this is how it happens with me.
I don't know what it will be until He tells me.
Then I learn what the message will be.

That is what happened today you see.
After dinner and the dishes were done.
I've had a burden on my heart all day.
The hope that each of us will now act as one.

Each and every one of us has a part to play.
In what the final outcome is to be.
A message will come from within our hearts.
Just rest in His presence the answer to see.

The Lord is with us here in this place.
The sun will shine on our faces again.
He will safely guide us through this trial.
We have only to call on His precious name.

THE WAY TO WORK

The Lord was riding with me today,
In His very special way.
He had His hand on the wheel,
And kept me from going astray.

The Lord was riding with me today,
And had His hand on the brake.
He protected me from an errant one,
And the mistake that I could make.

The Lord was riding with me today.
He did not let me lose my way.
Always keeping me from harm.
Holding me by grace yet another day.

The Lord was riding with me today.
I see no reason to be surprised.
I am never left alone,
And for this He should be praised.

The Lord rides with me every day.
I can always feel His care and love.
It's not a matter of when or where.
I just accept it, it's from above.

THE PASSING STORM

The day after the storm is bright and clear.
Everything around me is peaceful and still.
The trees move gently in the soft breeze.
The earth seems content to be under His will.

The night before was loud and frightening,
With roaring wind and driving rain.
Prayers were said seeking the Lord's comfort.
His presence was shown to me once again.

No matter what ever may happen to me.
If I sit quietly, His soft voice I will hear.
He will come to me through the storm.
Bestow His peace and take away my fear.

Today I look out my window and thank Him,
For all He does for me each and every day.
Why should I allow myself to worry?
He quietly walks with me all along the way.

THE SCALES OF YOUR LIFE

Sometimes you win, sometimes you lose.
Somehow it always seems to even out.
There will be good and then there's bad.
That's what this old world is all about.

You must simply be patient and understand,
Who is in control and what He will see.
The way will not always be clear for you.
Whatever happens is how it should be.

You must remember you are not the judge.
Things will be handled with His care.
He knows just where your heart is,
And that controls how things come to bear.

The way you act and your self-control,
Is what influences what He will do.
Do not let Satan control your thoughts.
And prevent Jesus from helping you.

Start each day asking for help from above,
And before you anger and go astray,
Slow down and think what really matters.
He will be there to help you find the way.

THE CROSS

I have everlasting hope and peace.
Because my Jesus was crucified.
He did not give a second thought.
He was wounded, he bled, and he died.

We are not supposed to understand,
Why he did this for us on that day.
We certainly did not deserve it,
But God knew it would happen that way.

All you ever need to do to thank him,
For what he did on the cross for you.
Is just accept him as your savior,
Then you can stand holding to his truth.

You may only have one chance in life,
To accept him as your very own.
Do not take it for granted,
Then he will return and take you home.

NEVER

Never get to where you think you have done enough
And there can be no more for you to do.
There will always be someone who needs your love,
Or just a small tender touch to see them through.

Never get to where you think there is no one to reach.
There is always somewhere else you need to go,
In order to find the ones who are lost out there.
They are out in the world and Jesus they do not know.

Never get to where you think you know it all.
There is always more of God's word you can read.
Then if only you are willing to listen, He will tell you,
Just where it is you need to let Him lead.

Never get to where you think He cannot use you.
There are so many things that are yet to be done.
You have something unique that He gave you.
Just be willing to use it, you are His special one.

Never get to where you think you don't have time.
Remember to ask Him, He can find a way for you.
He will give you the strength you will need each day.
He will hold you up and then you can see it through.

Never get to where you think you cannot forgive,
No matter how much you feel the pain.
Until you ask Him to help put it behind you,
Will you ever be able to find peace as your gain.

THE PEACEFUL WORD

Reading God's word can lift your spirits,
And then put you back on track.
It will show you where you need to be,
In order to get your perspective back.

Reading God's word lets you know,
That someone else has been there too.
So just look in His word for a message,
The one that the Lord has for you.

Reading God's word can bring such peace,
When things are constantly going astray.
So find a quiet, comfortable place to be,
Then be still and let Him show the way.

Reading God's word is not a chore.
It is a wonderful thing we are told to do.
It will tell you just how much he cares,
And allow Him to comfort you

Reading God's word can slow you down,
So you have the time to find your way.
To understand what needs to be done,
To turn the worst into a perfect day.

SMILING ANGELS

There is one less tear in heaven today.
What was prayed for has come to be.
One more name in the book of life.
Another soul from sin has been set free.

It's just one more of the amazing things,
That has happened to brighten our days.
The way it happened was in His plan.
We must now give the Lord the praise.

Because of this we must move forward.
There is still more work to be done.
Do not let us rest on unearned laurels.
We must still reach out to the errant one.

What has happened will give us courage.
There is no limit to what He can do.
Continue to pray and seek his guidance.
Use patience and love he will give to you.

Pray ever for faith and understanding.
Ask for the opportunity to lead the way,
Then let Him do what he will do best.
And then be ready for that saving day.

YOU HAVE ALWAYS BEEN THERE

Lord, please do not let me worry,
I need to have faith in your care.
I need to just wait and rest now.
I know You will always be there.

But since I live here in this world.
And it is sometimes hard not to let go.
But then You have always been there,
And just looking around tells me so.

I will tell my friends to pray for me,
That I will find peace in Your light.
And when this trial is finally over,
All my worries will have taken flight.

Maybe I just need to rest and wait,
So I get my life back in line with You.
How I handle this will influence others,
Who are watching to see what I do.

This You can certainly take care of.
And no matter what happens to me.
I will know You have always been there,
And when I look back this I will see.

That will be the answer to my prayer.

THE MEETING PLACE

Let me tell you about my Jesus.
I could not survive without His love.
I do not know where I would be,
Without His grace given from above.

There is no trial that I can have,
That He will not show the way to me.
He will hold me up and keep me safe,
And from my burdens set me free.

Wherever each day my life may take me.
I do not ever travel the road alone.
I may see no earthly sign that He is there.
I just know He is willing to be the one.

You only need to be open to His message.
It may come in many different ways.
It will give you direction for your life,
And guard you paths for all your days.

There is no place He has not been.
There is no road you need to fear.
Wherever you are He will be with you.
I know my Jesus will meet you there.

THE SAVING DAY

She came to tell me early this morning,
That last night she accepted our Lord.
That her life forever has changed,
Now her faith comes from His Holy Word.

There was that gladness in her heart,
That nothing can ever take away.
That now she goes directly to the Father,
And He will abide with her from this day.

Lord, let each of us who are her friends,
Always be there to support and uphold.
Let us be quiet so we can listen to her.
Saved by Jesus when His story was told.

This is a wonderful new life she has started.
Every day will be better than the one before.
Never again will she have to question.
The Father will hold her safe and secure.

WHO IS THIS CHURCH

How much can this church possibly mean to you?
How many souls can you show the way?
How many lives can you change for the better?
How many hearts can you give a brighter day?

How much can this church possibly mean to you?
It's going to take a lot of sweat and tears.
It's going to take time away from your family,
But then what will it accomplish over the years?

How many souls can you show the way?
This is a place where they will learn to live.
It must be a place where God can dwell.
There will be peace here only He can give.

How many lives can you change for the better?
There will be days you will be put to the test.
You don't really have any other options.
This is your calling; you must do your best.

How many hearts can you give a brighter day
As you accomplish what you look forward to?
Remember when everything is said and done,
Our God above will share this joy with you.

Never forget in the end, this is just a building!
Together you are to be a body of His stewards.
As He will lead you, use the building to His glory,
Then He will allow you to accept all His rewards.

WHAT WOULD JESUS DO

What would Jesus do
If it were left to Him to decide?
Can there be any doubt?
If it is right, He is on your side.

Would you call on Him to help
If your pathway was not clear?
Just take the time to think about it.
He wants to walk with you here.

Jesus finds joy in leading you.
He already knows what is to be.
He waits for you to call His name,
So His answer can set you free.

Do not ever lose your faith.
It is always yours to hold on to.
It is only part of the gift,
That He died to give to you.

THE GIFT

SALVATION

I got this gift some years ago.
It came at a very special time.
All my life I will remember the day.
It was from a special friend of mine.

It has comforted me over the years,
When life was not treating me fair.
In my heart I always remembered,
How the one who gave it cared.

I carry it with me all the time.
I would never want to give it away.
It was created especially for me.
I enjoy it each and every day.

One just like it could be yours.
It is something you will always need.
It can be sent free of charge.
Satisfaction is always guaranteed.

There will never be a shortage.
The version is always the same.
It is such a priceless acquisition.
To get yours, just call Jesus' name.

WHAT WOULD LOVE DO

Somehow the world has gone astray.
This is not how the Master wants it.
Wonder what some love would do,
If you gave it away as He sees fit?

It may not be that we can fix it all.
That does not mean that we give up.
Wonder what some love would do,
If we put some in the beggars' cup?

There are those who are lost and lonely,
Scattered all over our great land.
Wonder what some love would do,
With just the caring touch of a hand?

Do not ever think you cannot help,
To make this world a better place.
Wonder what some love would do,
You can share because of His grace?

Let your lamp be a light to others,
Who may need just a gentle touch.
Wonder what some love would do?
No way to measure just how much.

So go your way and live your life,
Trying to do what you think best.
Wonder what some love would do?
Stop and think; this could be a test.

THINGS

I find myself praying all day long.
This always puts my heart at rest.
It may be something very little,
Or maybe so I can just do my best.

I pray when I just need assurance,
That somehow everything will be okay.
Even when I don't know what's wrong.
Maybe it's just a cloudy, dreary day.

I pray for little things every day.
It is always something that I need.
This morning I prayed for my dog.
She gets sick when she's off her feed.

After all she is one of his creatures.
He made her to give us pleasure.
It will be our job to take care of her.
She repays us in no small measure.

This is fellowship with the Master.
He doesn't care what we pray for.
More important that we are praying,
So we will grow in Him all the more.

OPEN FOR BUSINESS

I saw the sign coming home from work,
Out by the road for everyone to see.
It is a business that's open on Sunday,
To make it easier for you and me.

They have to advertise so all will know,
Of interesting things that can be found.
They try to be better than the competition.
They are afraid they are losing ground.

They try many things to get our attention.
They say what they offer is better than most.
They are an equal opportunity employer.
There is always someone out front as a host.

They are open some evenings all year long,
So everyone can find a suitable time,
To come and see what they have to offer.
Whatever you need you will be able to find.

This place is easy to find and there are many.
Here they practice the great commission.
It is the church on the corner or down the road.
Open on Sunday and there is no admission.

GREAT BENEFITS

A LIVING CHURCH

With all things considered, not a bad group to join.
As this sort of establishment comes to mind.
There are those who search for a very long time.
Before something this good they are able to find.

As a member you are pretty much your own boss.
You only have to answer to the one at the top.
The guidelines are not really that hard to follow.
Just certain things to be done before you stop.

But then everyone needs a small bit of structure,
In order to get the important tasks properly done.
Suggestions on the time and different methods.
Usually can be handled on a basis of one on one.

The benefits of this organization are tremendous.
Too many to mention and they change every day.
Consistent attendance at the meetings is important,
So essential matters are handled the proper way.

The dues for this organization are often decided,
By your conscience and your own ability to give.
After all the membership is offered free of charge.
With benefits decided by how you choose to live.

THE ANSWER

There are so many ways for us.
To fix things that cause us pain.
Friends and family can comfort.
God's Word is there time and again.

But having the frailties that we do,
We try to muddle along to get it done.
We worry and let it change our lives.
In the end, Satan has always won.

We take our stress out on loved ones,
But they don't know what to say.
All they want to do is offer their help,
As they try to make it a better day.

In the end it is always so senseless.
The way we will worry and complain.
When all we have to do is ask Him
And He will be there once again.

You just don't have to deal with it.
You can leave it with the Lord tonight
He's going to be up all night anyway.
It won't take Him long to make it right.

TAKING CARE

Sometimes I have doubts and I will worry
And my eyes may even dim with tears.
But then He will make everything right.
He loves me, and He will remove my fears.

There are ways he watches over me,
Like just taking care of the daily things.
And giving me the peace and satisfaction,
That just trusting in Him always brings.

God's been good to me the last few days.
He's allowed me to help someone I love.
It's just another one of His blessings,
That comes on a regular basis from above.

A BOX OF MEMORIES

I've been going through a box of pictures,
And times and places come to mind.
As I continue sorting them out,
I know a lot of memories I will find.

There are those that lend to earlier days,
When life was at a more hectic pace.
But then there were such good times,
My mind returns me to that place.

The mountains where beauty abounds.
God's serenity and peace are found.
I'm going back there this summer,
To enjoy the river's sight and sound.

I remember sunrises out over the lake.
These scenes will never leave my mind.
I know things have changed since I left,
But there will be friends for me to find.

It is a good journey I will be taking,
And memories will be added to the chest.
I will return to share them with you.
The ones I'm making now will be the best.

THE QUIET CROSS

Today I saw a shadow on my porch,
Created by the warm morning sun.
Against the post that hold my roof,
To be a message for the days to come.

To create this Easter masterpiece,
Special events had to fall in place.
The way the sun was shining there,
As I looked out my window at that time,

A sign out front that protects my home,
Put there for all that pass my way to see.
Along with the post that holds my porch,
Made a shadow put there just for me.

I'm sure it's been there every morning,
But I had never seen it as such before.
Or the reason I looked out my window,
To find a message just outside my door.

A perfect cross found there on my porch,
Let's me know that a sign can be found.
That He walks and talks with me every day,
And he visits my soul without a sound.

GOD WITH US

THE ACCIDENT

The fact that He was there with us.
Has now brought us home to you.
It must be that He still needs us.
There is something left for us to do.

There may have been a time for us.
As His children we felt lost and alone.
Not knowing what was in store for us,
Yet His wonderful love was known.

He came to us in the late night hour,
When there was no earthly friend to find.
To keep us sheltered from a lonely world.
As our Father He would be gently kind.

There were those who went the extra mile,
And there were things only we could do.
Family came to give us comfort and aid.
With God's help brought us home for you.

So now you must continue to pray for us.
For health, healing, patience, and love.
As we now find the peace and contentment.
Which can only come from God above.

THE HEALING

RECOVERY

Things have started to settle a bit,
As we find our way to get things done.
Now all we have to do is get him better.
Knowing help from our Lord will come.

We must take each day as it comes,
As a blessing from our Lord above.
Knowing sure that we are only here,
Because of His unending grace and love.

We do not have to know the reason.
That would not change the story.
There are things best left unknown.
There is no accomplishment in worry.

Our prayer must be for acceptance,
Of what our Lord has in store.
Maybe we should be an example,
So He can bless us all the more.

Please stand near and watch for us,
As we find the way we should go.
Pray for us because your heart cares,
Then peace and comfort we will know.

COMPUTER ON LOAN

I can let you in on a little secret,
About this ability I have to write.
I always knew it was not all my doing.
Last night I think I saw the light.

This talent does not surprise my friends.
To put words on paper that will rhyme.
Sometimes it is not always that easy
Usually I have to wait for His time.

Then He tells me what He wants me to say,
And the sentences will start to flow.
They come to me, I write them down.
Most times the end result I do not know.

So last night it was quiet and I lay thinking,
Of how all things have a place and time.
I just let God above borrow my computer.
That's why the message is not always mine.

ANNA'S DOOR

The time is nearing for Anna's open door,
And we have been given a task to do.
We are awed as we step into God's presence.
But with His help, we will see it through.

Right now we can only give her comfort,
To make her path as peaceful as we can.
We stand near and wait for God's message,
So in the end our hearts will understand.

It will not be our choice of when or how.
Only God knows His master plan.
God will give the guidance we will need,
As He shelters her with His hand.

Answer our prayers as we wait on you.
Support us with your patience and love.
Give us blessed rest when we grow weary.
Knowing comfort comes from God above.

Your angels will gather with her at her door.
Then You will gently welcome her home.
She will never again have to suffer.
She will have peace she has never known.

PART OF A TASK

Another message came to me today.
Why I feel God gave me this task.
In this I will find the true satisfaction,
As He often gives me, I need not ask.

There is no way I could every repay Him,
For the blessings God gives me each day.
How He gave healing and blessed comfort,
Now a chance to help another find the way.

I do not have fear of what is to come.
I am awed that He would consider me.
One who has been where others walk.
To be found worthy of what is to be.

If I grow weary, He will lift me up again.
He will give me words to say and write.
It may come to be that I will be the one,
Able to hold a hand in the dark of night.

But if it is someone else's place to be,
I will know I have well done my part.
That what I did was just as important,
In God's plan to give ease to a heart.

COMMANDMENTS

I read in the newspaper just this morning.
They limit the place and when we pray.
How over the years we have lost sight,
And allowed them to take our rights away.

Our God gave us His rules to live by.
For centuries they have kept us true.
But by man's law we must keep them hidden,
In public I cannot display them for you.

Founding fathers divided church and state,
So the state had no cause to interfere.
With our right to pray to our Holy Father,
But rules to protect are no longer here.

They can post a copy of the Bill of Rights,
At any location for everyone to see.
Or even a copy of the US Constitution,
And it's approved because they are history.

If the Commandments are not history,
Then certainly there is a lot for us to fear.
Because in my heart there is no doubt,
They were sent by God, I hold them dear.

CROSS BEAUTY

There are few things that do not have beauty.
Each in its own right and for its own reason.
Some things are beautiful each and every day,
And some are only beautiful for their season.

It all depends on how much it matters to you,
And how you hold its meaning in your heart.
For the cross the beauty is often overshadowed,
By the use, which was to be hateful and dark.

The cross in my mind has a place of honor.
It is a constant reminder of who died for me.
It is made of oak and shines in splendor,
Up behind the pulpit for everyone to see.

Yet I always think of the pain and suffering,
Jesus endured on another cross so long ago.
It was blood stained and pierced with nails
I am truly amazed that He could love me so.

There is no way I can ever hope to repay Him.
And that will never be expected of you and I
There was never a doubt that He would do it.
He would never even ask His Father why.

LOST IN THE VALLEY

They saw me standing outside of my faith,
And bad that could happen was all I could see.
They promised me that God was in control.
Whatever happened He would stay with me.

I searched for peace that I could not find.
I lost my way and looked in the wrong place.
What I wanted was all that I could ask for.
What came to be was the result of His grace.

The prayers of my loved ones were answered.
They knew what was needed and asked for me.
They loved me and did not judge my faults.
They knew in their hearts what I failed to see.

The mountaintop is now again ours to claim.
God has led us through this valley for a reason.
Maybe I needed to remember how I needed Him,
And that everything will happen in a season.

When I look back I know we were never alone.
Friends and family prayed and held us tight.
They stood by and sheltered us with love
And held us in their hearts through the night.

AS THE LILY GROWS

As one walks through this life things happen,
And I have been in a valley for many a day.
Yet I have known some peace and comfort.
I am praying for my God to lead the way.

Over the next few days things may change.
My prayer must be that God's will be done.
I know He will stand with us and hold us up.
Even if we find there is a battle to be won.

I remember last year on Easter Sunday.
There was a beautiful lily up front for all to see.
Little did I know that after Sunday service,
This symbol of Easter would be given to me.

You remember you were my prayer sister,
And this was your special gift for me.
I planted it in our backyard when it faded.
I found it last month growing tall and free.

Whatever happens over the next few days,
I know that by this time next week.
That lily will bloom in all its splendor.
As I look at it, there will be comfort to seek.

ARC OVER THE CLOUD

I was out in my front yard this afternoon,
 Walking in the cooler part of the day.
 I just turned and looked up at the sky.
God had sent something beautiful my way.

Like something I had never seen before,
 Although my years are more than a few.
 I just happened to be there at that time,
 And God chose to give me that view.

A rainbow that surrounded a white cloud,
 As if it had been given a glorious crown.
 A clap of thunder had got my attention,
And now a thing of beauty had been found.

Like He chose to make "my" day a bit better,
 To put something there just for me to see.
Just over my house and shadowing my yard,
 To let me know He is never far from me.

God does good things for us every day.
 We just must be able to see His beauty.
 It is not as if we should have a choice.
 If we love Him, we will accept the duty.

THE SHEPHERD'S CARE

When I look at my life, it is no different,
Than most of those I see around me.
I have worked hard, I have paid my dues.
I feel I am where God wants me to be.

My life is pleasant in earthly things.
I can do what I want when I want to.
I have no schedule I have to meet.
When I need to, I can find time for you.

I do not dress to impress those I meet.
I'm wearing clothes I have had for years.
They still fit, are not ragged or torn.
I am at ease when among my peers.

Sometimes my attitude needs adjustment.
Those around me can always let me know.
Yet I am no different than most of you.
The best of me may not always show.

My health is good for my lot in life.
I have important things under control.
My doctor still shakes his head a lot.
But with his help I may even grow old.

I have learned that friends are important.
They will comfort you in the dark of night.
In order to have a friend you must be one.
Always work to keep this goal in sight.

Another thing that is important of late,
That no matter where this life may take me,
Patience and love will make the difference.
Resting in God's care is where I want to be.

My Father has put me in green pastures.
His still waters ever comfort my soul.
I want my life to be a beacon for others.
To accept His rewards shall be my goal.

THE CHRIST

There has been so much said of late,
On how our Jesus suffered and died.
How He was mocked and tortured,
After he was betrayed and then tried.

Not one follower stood to defend Him.
His judge could not save Him in the end.
Lots were cast for His only possessions.
He had been denied by His closest friend.

Those He came to earth to deliver,
Condemned Him to death on a cross.
He prayed for their souls with dying breath;
It mattered not; He gladly paid the cost.

For days He lay in a borrowed tomb,
But death could not win the victory.
He arose and ascended to His Father,
After promising to return for you and me.

This story has been told for centuries,
And it will never lose the healing touch.
No matter what the world may say to you,
Only your Jesus could love you that much.

AGAIN

Again our prayers have been answered.
A valley conquered, another battle won.
Again the mighty work God can do,
If we pray in the name of Jesus, His Son.

Again reminded of just who is in control.
How He uses others to accomplish a task.
Again a doctor and nurses do their work
To provide for your needs when you ask.

Again a pastor who has time just for you.
And the calls of friends that ease your heart.
Again there for you when you need them
Pray for you as you get a brand-new start.

Again able to be back at what you do best.
Quietly working every day in your own way.
Again allowed to be a witness of the power,
Of prayer and walking with God every day.

Again thankful for the valley we walked.
That the mountaintop is now ours to see.
Again someone just may find the way.
By the example God has allowed us to be.

PATH OF A CHURCH

I watched this building come into being,
By hard work, from a patch of weeds and grass.
From a distance I saw results of a strong few,
That with a God-given strength, finished the task.

We had a part in the growth of this building.
It was a labor of love that God gave us to do.
There was never a doubt it would come to be.
We were never discouraged; we just always knew.

We are now walking on a brand-new path.
One being directed by a gracious God above.
We have work to do to see it accomplished,
But we walk with the assurance of His love.

There will be trials and tribulations to come,
And that is perhaps how it should be.
Because we will grow in the face of diversity.
And what we do now is for the world to see.

The growth of a church depends on the people,
That God places on the path they must thread.
It should not be that the few will do it all.
Just rewards will come from a thankful God.

A church consists of praying men and women,
Who by their actions accomplish a common goal.
Who will always live and labor in God's word,
So in the end a story of victory can be told.

KATRINA'S WRATH

Today I saw the awesome power of nature,
And it is but for the grace of God that go I.
There is no need to search for an answer.
In our life we will never know a reason why.

It must be our lot to be in constant prayer,
For those who survived this tragic event.
That God will uphold and sustain them,
And comfort when tired bodies are spent.

He must give them the strength they need,
To survive the unknown trials and fear.
Knowing that at this terrible time in life,
If they ask in His name, He will surely hear.

I pray that families who never find loved ones,
Can find peace from the strength of His Grace.
And know that God has taken them into His fold,
And they are forever secure in a better place.

Be in prayer for those who risk their lives to help.
God will provide courage and strength they need.
That they will return safely to their loved ones,
From a task they will have done well indeed.

JUST HOW MANY

There are so many bad things of late.
So many lives are in utter despair.
Many have lost everything they owned,
And wonder if there is anyone to care.

Many may never find their loved ones.
What happened only heaven will know.
Many have nothing left on earth to hold to.
They have no direction as to where to go.

There are many prayers being said today,
And many to be spoken in the days ahead.
For some, it will be the only hope they have,
That He promised to provide their daily bread.

There are those who are constantly praying,
For strength people need to make another day.
Hour after hour and prayer after prayer.
That hope and a vision will come their way.

Just how many prayers will God hear today?
Do not doubt He will hear each reverent plea.
Just remember how He answers the prayer,
Will be what is best, and it will come to be.

DAILY

Lately I've been taking stock of life,
And how things have evolved of late.
How my life just seems to fall in place,
Without a worry about time or date.

There are days when I find myself busy,
And don't know how, when, or where.
But mostly I can just reflect on my life,
And thank my Lord for his daily care.

I still have those I must think about,
And let these thoughts be a request.
This is an arrangement with my Lord,
If I say their name, He will do what's best.

I am thankful He gives me things to do,
That will reflect His magnificent love.
It is my pleasure to witness for Him.
That what I do is guided from above.

I am no different from anyone else.
This is how the Lord wants us to live.
We can each have a part to play
In the blessings our Lord will give.

GOD'S CO

FINISHED BUILDING

They have told us that we passed the test.
What we set out to do has been accomplished.
The work was often hard, but we made a promise.
The sense of reward is far more than we wished.

We have received praise of friends and family.
We feel they are proud of all that has been done.
And many who prayed and helped with the work.
We must hope the result is that souls will be won.

People gave time that could have been with family.
But it needed to be done; it was a God-given task
They were bone weary when the work day ended.
They started the next day without being asked.

The results of the labor belong to our Lord.
Those who labored, He will reward each of them.
It was an opportunity for which we are grateful.
All that was accomplished now belongs to Him.

The result is a gift for use in the Lord's work.
We are proud of what we were allowed to do.
Whatever good comes from this is in His honor.
Its care is now the responsibility of each of you.

FAITH'S LEGACY

Right now you have God's personal attention.
I know there is no safer place for you to be.
Therefore you should not look for a reason.
In due time His message you will surely see.

Anything I could do will pale in comparison.
You already have our prayers and love.
Now you must depend completely on Him,
For the comfort that can only come from above.

But I will abide quietly in the background.
I will be here for you just outside your gate.
If there is anything I can do, He will tell me.
It will be my task to just stand and wait.

Strangers will hold you next to their hearts.
They will reach for you quietly every day.
They will ask our Father in heaven above,
To touch your life and show the way.

God will add to the strength you already have.
This will support you as you walk this road.
Though you may feel alone and heavyhearted.
Jesus is there to help you to carry this load.

What I have told you is with good authority.
I have relied on this faith to hold me for years.
And now it will move from His heart to yours.
And you can use Jesus' shoulder to dry your tears.

THAT'S HOW MY HEART WRITES

I often wonder what the words will say,
When something is heavy on my heart.
There comes a time when I cannot wait.
Whatever will happen I have to start.

He allows me to comfort my fellow man,
And make his load easier to carry.
This is a blessing that awes my mind,
And I will lose the message if I tarry.

Many times it is meant to comfort someone,
Who has a burden that's hard to bear.
Or maybe it's that I'm far away from them,
And only in my heart can I be there.

Or maybe it is I who needs the comfort,
And it is His way of letting me know.
That He still holds me near His heart,
And He will show the way for me to go.

Do not think I am the one with the talent,
It is not my doing that will show you a light.
That if in my mind a message should come,
God tells my heart what it should write.

OF LATE

This message has taken me days to write.
My heart finds it harder to deal with grief.
There are so many more people to pray for.
That deep in their hearts they will find relief.

There have been so many bad things of late,
People dying for no accountable reason.
Hearts are broken and lives forever changed.
I realize that tragedy does not have a season.

I find I must deal with my own sad ghosts,
When it comes to what I should do or say.
Just maybe that is how it is meant to be.
If you have been there, you can find a way.

Years of dealing with life's deep valleys,
Has given insight to how deep grief can go.
And how what you say to the grieving,
Is so important if comfort they will know.

Sometimes I know no word or verse to say,
But I do know that in the end God is there.
Sometimes you just have to turn it over.
They will never be safer than when in His care.

HEARTS FAR AWAY

So much is happening to you just now.
Things I have no way to make right
It's like I'm just too far away to help.
I cannot see you in the cold dark night.

If I were there, I would quietly open my door,
And I would put your head on my shoulder
I would let you rest with me for a while.
Get your strength back and be a bit bolder.

I would pray with you and give you comfort.
A cup of coffee and we would just sit and rest.
There would be nothing to do or place to go.
We would trust our Lord to do what is best.

Maybe I would just sit and talk with you,
And let the world out there pass us by.
Or maybe just not speak any words,
And we would not have to know just why.

I can do none of this for you right now.
I must just abide down here and pray.
That my Heavenly Father will hold you,
And help you through the coming day.

Know in your heart that I am with you.
Feel my hand on your saddened face.
There is no comfort like answered prayer.
God will support you by His loving grace.

THE MASTER'S CARD

Today I used the master's card again.
This time I used it to make a payment.
You see I thanked Him for something;
For a wonderful blessing He had sent.

He gave it to me when I accepted Him,
And now I enjoy the peace of mind.
Knowing it will never be rejected.
I can use it for His works at any time.

There is no interest on this account.
It is available twenty-four hours a day.
I carry it in my heart, it's just for me.
I can use it for a map if I lose my way.

I do not have to sign this card.
I furnish no ID, He knows my name.
He manages my account in His time.
A payment or charge is all the same.

I've always had this card to use.
It goes with me everywhere I need to.
It always has an unlimited balance.
I use it daily, yet the bill is never due.

You do not need to apply to get one.
It's yours if you ask from your heart.
For the healing touch you will need,
To get up and make a brand-new start.

PRAYER LIST

Today I did what you told us to do.
I will have it with me wherever I go.
Now I know what I must not forget.
I will keep a record so I will know.

I turned my petitions over to Him.
That is where they must always be.
I must leave them there in His care,
If contentment I can ultimately see.

Immediately my mind began to rest.
It's as if I wrote it down just for Him.
Now we can talk until we get it done,
And I know He will take care of them.

I know I must rely on God-given faith,
To hold me in the trials I will face.
That He knows what is best for me,
And I will find rest in His loving grace.

I know you will keep us in your prayers,
And there will be no parting of our ways.
As we travel together down life's road,
You will be one who shares our days.

MOVING INTO FALL

The seasons are changing here in Georgia.
The days are shorter, the trees are turning.
Mornings are cooler and days not so warm.
It is something for which I have been yearning.

Yards decorated with pumpkins and scarecrows.
The maple will be a beautiful green and gold.
Our home will be cozy because of the fireplace.
It brings to mind stories that have been told.

God has taken care of us in so many ways,
And we know there is a reason it came to be.
This was a year we didn't know would happen.
Another one of His plans that we would see.

He has given us great things to do for Him.
And friendships that daily warm our heart.
He just moved us from one place to another,
And allowed us to have a brand-new start.

Old friends dwell in special corners of a heart.
In the mind's eye you will see a sweet face.
And memories we made will be kept forever.
They will dwell in an extraordinary place.

PSALM 91

Today in my Mother's Bible I found it.
What will sustain us in the coming days.
If we believe on this message from God,
We will find comfort and peace in His ways.

This chapter will be our sustainer in trials.
We can always find hope and peace there.
In the quiet times of our days and nights,
It will certainly be our comforting prayer.

The Father again answered our prayers.
The top of the mountain is ours to claim.
Again Satan could not win the battle.
Thanks must go up in our Jesus' name.

I share this with you because I need to.
I am told to love and help my fellow man.
I hope this can make your day brighter,
And He will shelter you under His hand.

So if you are struggling to find your way,
And Satan makes the battle hard to win.
A lesson can be learned to ease the pain.
Jesus is here, He loves you, you win again.

A PLACE AND TIME

I went home to where my roots were formed,
A visit to a church where salvation was free.
Many years ago yet the memory is still strong,
A gift from God that cannot be taken from me.

I saw the house where I spent my younger years,
Although it has changed never to be the same.
But that's okay you see, visions are still with me,
A different time, a different place, different name.

There were those who remembered my youth,
I spent time with family members that are there,
And we shared memories known only to a few.
Best friends still abound, and I know they care.

I am back home in Georgia, safe and secure.
I have a special place in my heart just for you.
I will promise to come back to see you again,
And I will try to make this promise come true.

I am at peace; I am where God wants me to be.
I work for Him because He leads me every day.
He has put me here because He has work for me.
I am confident that He will show me the way.

WHERE I AM NOW

I could not be here where I am today,
Without having been with you those years.
It was God's plan that I should be there.
There was hard work, sweat, and tears.

It was His plan to make me a better person.
One who could serve Him in another place.
I learned how hard work is appreciated,
When you are depended on to keep the pace.

There are things that I have learned to do.
I use talents that have always been mine.
And they were perfected when I was there,
In the background, waiting for me to find.

Do not feel sad we are no longer with you.
Everyone is where God wants them to be.
We all have a place in the scheme of things.
Just patiently wait and you will surely see.

Think of me often in the prayers you pray,
As prayers I pray will certainly be for you.
I know it is because I was there at that time,
The Heavenly Father gave me the work I do.

THE SUNDAY SERMON

Lord, you just seem to take care of things,
And I fail even when I try will all my might.
It is my lot to do the best I can each day.
My prayers usually go up to You at night

When the night is quiet and I can't sleep,
I can remember all the things you did for me.
That made my day go just a little bit better,
Lord, look in my heart, thanks you will see.

Every day I have things I need from You,
And no one else on earth can fill the bill.
That it takes to see me through this life.
Mostly there is just no one else who will.

I could ask you to remind me to pray,
But that is not the way it should be.
Habits I have formed are my downfall.
I'll try to do better, just You wait and see.

This is a promise I made to myself,
From a sermon I heard the other day.
It told me how I should praise you,
And depend on You to lead the way.

So just be patient with me today, Lord.
By writing this I am thanking You again.
If I try harder a better path to walk,
Between the two of us, I just might win.

A PICTURE TAKEN

Today while walking I saw a picture,
In my mind only God could make.
It was there waiting for me to see,
Peace and comfort, mine to take.

So beautiful that it took my breath.
There was a message only for me.
It would give me a wonderful day.
God put it there just for me to see.

He does this for me all the time.
It's part of my daily walk with Him.
There are always messages for me.
When I talk with Him, I will see them.

I am often amazed where they are.
So easy to find as I walk and pray.
Out there for the whole world to see,
But more than that, to make my day.

One evening when alone with Him.
There was nothing for me to say.
This was a time He spoke to me.
And I'm going to live there one day

ON ELECTION DAY

It is my humble opinion that on this day,
The Heavenly Father will hear our voices,
More than ever in the history of my America.
Prayers that we will make the right choices.

It will come down to the final count.
We have to make a decision that is right.
We have to vote across the dividing line,
To keep the future of America in sight.

We will not have a second chance that day.
We have to get it right the very first time.
There will be no chance to do it over.
Hindsight will not be a comfort we find.

There is only one way to make it work
We must be in vigilant, earnest prayer,
That our God will cover and protect us,
As we make our decision in that hour.

BACK HOME AGAIN

I went back to summit while I was there,
To a house where roots were put down.
It will never be the same as it used to be,
But a place where memories are found.

I went back to where my parents rest.
It will always have a place in my heart.
I went there when the world was cold,
Or if I needed a softer place to start.

I traveled the roads of years gone by.
They did not take me to familiar places.
The changes are too many to number.
There were no longer friendly faces.

But I will remember my journey back,
And I met with some I had known before.
I can remember things that used to be,
And it was good to see them once more.

I learned a pleasant lesson on this trip.
There will always be something to find.
So you know you can go home again,
And make memories of a different kind.

BACKGROUND WORKERS

There are great people in everyone's lives.
They are put here by a higher being.
Often they stand alone in the wings,
Of life's stage without your ever seeing.

They go quietly about everyday tasks,
Helping those placed along their way.
They have an honored talent few will have.
Their goal is to give strength for your day.

You may only see them if they are needed,
When it is necessary to be there for you.
To take care of whatever troubles your life,
To give direction as to what is best to do.

You know when needed they will be there.
God put them here to take care of you.
It does not matter if you are rich or poor.
They go the extra mile because they want to.

All the attributes you see listed above,
Are only a few of what should be told.
Because that is what they wanted to do
Good works are more precious than gold.

THOUGHTS OF THINGS

It's been a while since this pain was mine,
But I remember how it felt that day.
Something was lost I would never recover,
One of those things that marks your way.

You will find comfort knowing she is safe,
That she will not have to suffer anymore.
That you will see her again someday.
You have many memories you can store.

You have friends and family nearby,
Just waiting for some way to comfort you.
But mostly it is your time to mourn.
God's grace and mercy will see you through.

All of life's experiences are for a reason.
Maybe just to be able to help another.
So when their time comes to bear,
You know how it is to lose a mother.

You will go onward with peace of mind.
You completed a task and you can tell,
You were a good daughter to the end.
This is a memory that will do you well.

WEATHER IN A DOUGHNUT HOLE

In Florida you just look out the window,
And see what the weather is doing.
I do not know where our forecaster is.
There have been times I thought of suing.

They take the blame for a lot of things,
And I know they are educated well.
But right here in our little doughnut hole,
Leave me alone, my weather I can tell.

You see I've learned about their flaws.
For the temperature just add five degrees.
If a storm is brewing, and I don't see a cloud,
I look at the sky but don't know what he sees.

When they tell us it will be bright and clear,
You can keep an umbrella in your car.
If you go by what they say will happen,
You can't run to the car, it's just too far.

If they say it's going to rain on the parade,
Just take your chances you'll probably win,
After all, the natives will tell you every day,
Look out the window, that's how it's always been.

If you find yourself out in a Florida shower,
Don't fight it, just plan on getting wet.
You cannot get into a car holding an umbrella.
A way to stay dry in a shower is not invented yet.